Conversations With Sharks

Success Secrets Shared By The Sharks On ABC's Hit TV Show Shark Tank

Strategies Extracted From Closed Door Interviews of Barbara Corcoran & Daymond John

By Kelly Cole

Legal Disclaimers

This Book is not in any way affiliated with ABC Shark Tank.

DEDICATION

This book is dedicated to my granddaddy, John Henry Pete. He was my first example of entrepreneurship. While working 2 to 3 jobs at a time he still managed to run his own businesses on the side. He sold pillows, whirl pools for the bath tub, and cookies to the local stores, plus he had several fruit stands. My favorite was his fruit stands. He used to let me & my cousins work with him in the summer for $3.00 a week. That was great money in the 80's, I felt like I had a million bucks in my pocket. I had enough to buy anything I wanted from the candy store. He was a great example of working hard and never giving up. I never once saw him discourage because something didn't work, he simply moved on to the next idea he had. I thank God he is still living today!

Thanks granddaddy for the inspiration to become an entrepreneur.

Love Your Grandson,
Kelly

Foreword

Often we hear people ask the question, "If you could spend an hour with a millionaire, what questions would you ask?" Really, what we are seeking are better ways to achieve a specific goal, dream or vision. The key is not waiting for that moment to present itself, but creating it.

I have known Kelly Cole for many years and have personally witness his passion and drive for success. It is evident in his daily walk in life, as he devours information from those who have reached the level of success he's aiming towards. Kelly doesn't wait for opportunities... he creates them. Even at times he must quiet his inner entrepreneur because of the array opportunities he desires to put into motion.

This book is one of those opportunities Kelly created. He took the desire and his idea to learn from those whom he has admired from afar to create one-on-one mentoring not solely for himself, but for others as well. Kelly has read their books and watched them weekly on ABC's Shark Tank. His thirst to learn is to the point where he watches the episodes of Shark Tank over and over. Just watching wasn't enough; Kelly wanted and needed to ask questions to gain a better understanding. If you're an entrepreneur then this book is a must read for you. No matter where you are in your business: a vision to 10 years, this book will definitely provide you with at least one "ah-ah" moment.

Conversations With Sharks gives you a bird-eyes view of the "how-to," "when-to" and "who-to" of Barbara Corcoran and Daymond John. These two moguls took their ideas, recognized as well as created opportunities for success. Barbara is very candied on how she started with a $1,000 loan. As for Daymond, his unique methods of reaching the masses with his international brand FUBU will make you think.

Not to spoil the book for you, however, Kelly really inspires you to get up and to get moving. He shares his experience of submitting his idea to Shark Tank and the process. You get behind the curtain access. He doesn't stop there. It's all about tapping into the mind of those who have reached a point on your quest for whatever level of success you desire within.

Well, it's time for you to pull out your pen, high-lighter, and pad as you consume the words of this book. Don't just read this book, Study this book! Open yourself to expect: enlightenment, a new idea, inspiration, and hope. So this means reading every page thoroughly. Doing what it says and following the advice of Kelly & The Sharks. It will change your life. It's time to step into the conversation, so that your business will become a conversation amongst others.

C.F. Jackson
www.EmailConnecting.com

CONTENTS

Be Sure And Download Your Free Bonuses Here:
www.conversationswithsharks.com/bonuses

Introduction

I got the idea to write this book after watching Shark Tank the first time. I was mesmerized by the art of negotiation and making a deal. I began recording every episode and taking loads of notes.

Then it came to me and I asked myself, "Why not turn this great info into a book?" I knew if I enjoyed all of the great nuggets the sharks were giving away, other entrepreneurs would too.

After I began writing this book I decided it would be great to be able to receive tips and strategies right from the Shark's mouth. So I began to reach out to them one by one, via their website and social media. To my surprise Barbara Corcoran's assistant responded to my email almost instantly. She asked me for a little more information about who I was and then went on to setup a date and time I could interview Barbara. Well a couple of days before I was to interview Barbara her assistant contacted me again, this time to reschedule because Barbara had some conflict with her schedule. We rescheduled and I was able to interview Barbara for about 45mins via telephone and let's just say Barbara and I hit it off almost instantly. I felt like I had known her all my life. It was great to interview her and for her to be so cool and humble.

Needless to say Barbara was the only one to who even respond to my request for an interview. But I remembered an old saying "It's not always what you know, but who you know!" By the end of Barbara and I's interview I felt so comfortable with her. I asked her if she would help me get an interview with Daymond John. She, without any hesitation, said yes. She gave me detail instructions on what to do and that she would pass it on to Daymond. I followed her instructions to a T, and she did exactly what she said she would and sent it over to Daymond and "BC" me in the email. She said "Daymond Please Give Him an Interview, He's A Great Guy" – just to read her say those words about me made me feel all warm and fussy inside. Even if Daymond didn't give me an interview, I felt good because Barbara and I connected. Well about 10mins after Barbara sent the email I got an email from Daymond instructing me on what to do to setup the interview. I was more than excited, Daymond was someone I'd looked up too for the majority of my life and to be able to interview him I knew my life would never be the same again.

Unlike when I interviewed Barbara it took a minute for Daymond to warm up. That could have been because I was so nervous or because it was early in the morning, anyhow I was just honored to be on the phone with him. After he warmed up, he began to pour knowledge into me not only about business but life in-general. I want to go on the record and say thank you to him and Barbara for taking out the time to bless me with an interview.

Inside this book you will benefit from not only the trials and tribulations of the Sharks but also learn the proper way to go about your business and the proper way to present it to investors.

What Is Shark Tank?

Shark Tank is a reality television series based on the Sony TV/BBC TV Dragons' Den. It premiered on ABC television in August 2009 and featured a panel of five wealthy entrepreneurs who were called "Sharks". The panel evaluates and negotiates investment proposals from entrepreneurs. The series is produced by Mark Burnett in conjunction with Dragons' Den format-holder Sony and has been compared to the ABC series American Inventor.

The panel consists of five business people called "Sharks". Each panel member has the option of negotiating and investing with an entrepreneur who has presented a product, service or business concept. Panel members may offer investment capital, support and expertise, or they may make an offer to buy the company, or the product license or patent.

Panel members include:

Barbara Corcoran, **Real Estate Tycoon, The Corcoran Group.**

This big bucks self-starter's credentials include straight D's in high school, college and 20 jobs by the time she'd turned 23. Don't believe us?

Now what would you say if we told you it was Barbara Corcoran's next job that would make her one of the most successful entrepreneurs in the country? She borrowed $1,000 from her boyfriend and quit her job as a waitress to start a tiny real estate company in New York City.

3

Over the next 25 years, she'd parlay that $1,000 loan into a five-billion-dollar real estate business and the largest and best known brand in the industry.

As a speaker, Barbara brings her front-lines experience and infectious energy to each person in the audience. They laugh, cry and learn how to become more successful. Motivational, inspirational and sometimes outrageous, Barbara Corcoran's tell-it-like-it-is attitude is a refreshing approach to success.

The author of If You Don't Have Big Breasts, Put Ribbons on Your Pigtails, an unlikely business book that has become a national best-seller, Barbara credits her struggles in school and her mother's kitchen-table wisdom for her innovation and huge success in the business world. The book is a fresh look at how to succeed in life and business, and is as heartwarming as it is smart and motivating.

Barbara is the popular real estate contributor for the Today Show and CNBC. She writes a weekly real estate column for the Daily News and monthly columns for MORE Magazine and Redbook. In 2008, she released her second book, Nextville: Amazing Places to Live the Rest of Your Life, to great reviews.

Daymond John, founder of the clothing company FUBU, Which earned $350 million in 1998.

Here's a true entrepreneur who keeps us dressed to the nines while we play hard on both field and walk down the path of life.

Daymond John's creative vision helped revolutionize the sportswear industry in the 1990s. As founder, president and chief executive officer of FUBU—"For Us, By Us"— Daymond created distinctive and fashionable sportswear and a host of other related gear. FUBU's phenomenal success made mainstream apparel companies realize the potential for fashionable sportswear that appeals not just too trendsetting urban youth, but to mainstream teens as well.

Daymond was born in the New York City borough of Brooklyn but spent his childhood in the Hollis neighborhood of Queens during the 1970s. As an only child, he grew up in a single-parent household headed by his mother, who was a flight attendant for American Airlines but often held more than one job. His first foray into the apparel market came when he wanted a tie-top hat and was put off by the price. Daymond asked his mother to teach him how to use a sewing machine, and he began making the distinctive tie-top hats in the morning and then selling them on the streets of Queens in the evening hours.

One day in 1992, he and his friend sold $800 worth of hats and realized their ideas had definite potential. They created a distinctive logo and began sewing the FUBU logo on hockey jerseys, sweatshirts and t-shirts. Daymond lured some longtime friends into the business and asked old neighborhood friend, L.L. Cool J., to wear a t-shirt in a photograph for a FUBU promotional campaign in 1993. Daymond and his mother mortgaged the home they collectively owned for the $100,000 in start-up capital. Even more amazingly, she then moved out so the quartet could use the home as a makeshift factory and office space.

FUBU officially emerged in 1994 when Daymond and his partners traveled to an industry trade show in Las Vegas. Buyers liked the distinctively cut, vibrantly colored sportswear, and Daymond and his partners returned to Queens with $300,000 worth of orders. FUBU soon had a contract with the New York City-based department store chain Macy's, and they began expanding their line to include jeans and outerwear. A distribution deal with Korean electronics manufacturer Samsung allowed their designs to be manufactured and delivered on a massive scale.

As CEO and president, Daymond guided FUBU to a staggering $350 million in revenues in 1998, placing it in the same stratosphere as such designer sportswear labels as Donna Karan New York and Tommy Hilfiger. Over the last 16 years, Daymond has evolved into more than a fashion mogul. In 2007 the street-smart businessman penned his first book, Display of Power: How FUBU Changed a World of Fashion, Branding & Lifestyle, which was named one of the best business books of 2007 by the Library Journal.

Known as the "Godfather of Urban Fashion," Daymond is regarded as one of the most sought-after branding experts and keynote speakers in fashion and business today. With multiple business ventures on his resume, Daymond can be seen sharing his knowledge and business genius on numerous business and entertainment television programs.

Robert Herjavec - Sold his first tech company for $100 million.

We all know the dot com industry has had its ups and downs over the past decade. But here's a guy who continually manages to bracket the boom with dollar signs!

Robert Herjavec has lived the classic "rags to riches" story. The son of Croatian immigrants, he earned his incredible wealth by overcoming the odds with pure hard work and intuition. He remembers how his mother, who could barely speak English, lost the family savings to a smooth-talking vacuum salesman. Since then, Robert vowed he would never let his family be taken advantage of again.

In the early '90s, Robert eked out a living by waiting tables at a posh Yorkville restaurant. During the initial stages of the dot com craze, he realized that technology was the ticket to serious money.

By night, he launched BRAK systems, his first technology company, which is now worth a reported $100 million dollars. He sold his company to AT&T in 2000, but that was only the start. Robert then helped negotiate the sale of another technology company to Nokia for $225 million. Instead of retiring with his cash, he now heads The Herjavec Group, a leading IT security and infrastructure integration firm.

His palatial 50,000 square foot Bridle Path mansion hosts luminaries like Michael Bublé and Mick Jagger. For thrills, Robert jets to a private island near Miami or cruises Yorkville in one of his many luxury cars.

Kevin O'Leary, Sold his company to Mattel for $3.7 billion. We think this guy is opinionated, ruthless, hungers for big deals and loves to take control—yet he made his millions helping children learn how to read.

Kevin O'Leary's success story starts where most entrepreneurs begin: with a big idea and zero cash. From his basement, he launched SoftKey Software Products. As sales took off, Kevin moved to headquarters in Cambridge, Massachusetts and went on an industry consolidating acquisition binge.

From 1995 to 1999 he bought out almost every one of his software competitors, including Mindscape, Broderbund and the Learning Company in the industry's first vicious public hostile battle. Shareholders loved his take-no-prisoners, cost cutting style and fueled him with billions to do his deals.

In 1999 Kevin sold his company to the Mattel Toy Company for a staggering 3.7 billion dollars, one of the largest deals ever done in the consumer software industry. To keep his money working hard, he took control of his wealth from his lackluster money managers and founded his own mutual fund company, O'Leary Funds. He raised hundreds of millions of dollars from investors who share his "get paid while you wait" yield oriented, value investing philosophy. He shares his tips and tribulations with a national television audience and turns The Street upside down in the process.

As a self-proclaimed "Eco-preneur," Kevin looks hardest for investments that make money - and are environmentally friendly. When he's not squeezing the market from his office in West Palm Beach, he travels the world looking for new opportunities to deploy his capital. He is a founding investor and director of Stream Global, an international business outsourcing company. He is on the investment committee of Boston's prestigious 200-year-old Hamilton Trust, and is the chairman of O'Leary Funds. He also serves on the executive board of The Richard Ivey School of Business.

Kevin escapes on weekends with his family to his luxurious cottage that spreads over prime Canadian wilderness on the shore of an ancient glacial lake.

Kevin Harrington, pioneer in the infomercial industry, His first company reached $500 million in annual sales.

Kevin Harrington, chairman and founder of TV Goods Inc., is a pioneer and principal architect of the infomercial industry. But we've come to know him as the sharp-looking shark seated at the left end of the tank.

In 1984, Kevin produced one of the industry's first 30-minute infomercials. Since then he has been involved with over 500 product launches that resulted in sales of over $4 billion worldwide, with 20 products that reached individual sales of over $100 million. Not bad. Not bad at all.

Kevin founded Quantum International, Ltd. in the mid-1980s, which merged into National Media Corporation in 1991. Under his leadership as President, National Media reached $500 million in annual sales, distributing in over 100 countries and 20 languages. This company's success has been chronicled in a case study at Harvard/MIT for over a decade.

Kevin was also CEO of several other entrepreneurial companies, including HSN Direct, a joint venture with Home Shopping Network in 1994 and Reliant International Media in 1997. Throughout his career, Kevin helped to establish two of the most important and recognized global networking associations, the Entrepreneur's Organization, or EO (formally known as the Young Entrepreneurs' Organization), and the Electronic Retailing Association, or ERA.

Today, the EO has 113 chapters in 38 countries and more than 924,000 members. The ERA represents the $125 billion electronic retailing industry and is comprised of over 450 member companies and subsidiaries that use the power of electronic retailing to sell directly to consumers via television, radio, Internet and wireless media in over 100 countries worldwide.

Kevin recently released a book entitled <u>Act Now: How I Turn Ideas into Million-Dollar Products</u> that chronicles his life and experiences in the DRTV industry. As you can see, Kevin is a fairly busy guy. But there's always time to make a few bucks gobbling up a good idea in the Shark Tank!

Mark Cuban, owner of the Dallas Mavericks, Landmark Theatres, and chairman of the HDTV cable network HDNet.

Mark Cuban was an entrepreneur from the early age of 12, when he sold garbage bags door-to-door. Today, Mark is the highly successful entrepreneur and investor who founded HDNet, Broadcast.com and MicroSolutions. He has also been an investor in startups, including Mahalo, JungleCents.com, motionloft.com, Filesanywhere.com, Naked Pizza and 140Fire.com.

Named a winner of the GQ "Men of the Year" in 2006 and included in the New York Times Magazine's "Year in Ideas," Mark is recognized as being among the most influential people in both the cable and sports industries.

Mark may be best known for his purchase of the Dallas Mavericks on January 4, 2000. Under his leadership, the team's home games have become a total entertainment experience. Despite initial criticism, he added much more to the usual game-day experience by introducing original video content, advanced technology and unique entertainment options like the Mavericks ManiAACs. His successful efforts have brought a sense of pride and passion to the fans.

Prior to his purchase of the Mavericks, Mark co-founded Broadcast.com, the leading provider of multimedia and streaming on the Internet. Broadcast.com was sold to Yahoo! Inc. in July 1999. MicroSolutions, a leading national systems integrator, was co-founded by Mark and partner Martin Woodall in 1983 and later sold to CompuServe.

Currently, Mark is the owner and chairman of HDNet (www.HD.net). HDNet and its sister network, HDNet Movies, are one of the few remaining independently owned and operated TV Networks in the U.S. and the first in the world to be programmed exclusively in high definition. Mark takes personal responsibility for the programming on both networks, creating a unique schedule of creative and original programs. Behind his leadership and that of his co-founder, Philip Garvin, HDNet continues to outperform networks owned by much larger corporations and those with much greater distribution.

Mark also co-owns the Landmark Theater chain, Magnolia Pictures and Magnolia Home Video along with partner Todd Wagner. With the release of the movie Bubble in 2005, Magnolia and Landmark Theaters pioneered the release of the movie's "Day and Date," meaning the movie was released in theaters, on TV (HDNet Movies) and on DVD all on the same day. Taking this process one step further, Mark created the "Ultra VOD" platform for movies, releasing movies to video-on-demand on both cable and satellite up to four weeks prior to their release in theaters.

Mark Cuban is used to riding the waves of success so he should be right at home swimming with the Sharks!

Jeff Foxworthy, Comedian Grammy Award winner, author and TV host.

A self-made successful businessman in his own right, Jeff Foxworthy expanded his popular work in stand-up comedy into an empire of albums, books, hit comedy tours, and forays into television and radio, including his work as host of Are You Smarter Than a 5th Grader?

Jeff is the largest selling comedy-recording artist of all-time. As an entrepreneur, he has a line of greeting cards and specialty products through American Greetings that are available at all Wal-Mart stores. He has a line of You Might Be a Redneck If... calendars which have sold millions of copies. He also has his own line of beef jerky, as well as a line of barbeque sauces. Well, sharks do like meat!

In October 2003, the Nevada Gaming Commission granted approval for Aristocrat Technologies, Inc. to place its Jeff Foxworthy™ You Might Be a Redneck If...® video slot games in Nevada casinos. Station Casinos, Inc. was granted the right to introduce Aristocrat's Jeff Foxworthy games into its 11 Las Vegas valley casino properties exclusively for 45 days prior to the game's release to other Las Vegas off-Strip casino properties.

It's not Vegas, but the Shark Tank is one place where Jeff may gamble on a bright new entrepreneur. The only sure bet is that Jeff will surely provide us with some laughs before the deal is done.

Shark Quote

"I never let emotions get in the way of an investment"
– Kevin O'Leary

How My 4yr Old Daughter & I Almost Got On Shark Tank!

Alove Cole aka Lovie, my 6yr old daughter, has her own business LovieLipGloss.com. I got the idea to create Lovie Lip Gloss when Alove was 2yrs old and started getting dressed with her mom. She developed a passion and a love for lip gloss so much so that she wouldn't leave the house without some on and often times if we got in the car and she didn't have any lip gloss on, we would have to turn around to go get it.

So one Christmas about two years ago she wanted lip gloss for Christmas and I said "hey, let's make her own lip gloss line." So I began to do the research on the process of making the line. At one period my wife and I bought materials to make it at home ourselves but it didn't turn out the way we wanted it, so we decided to look for a manufacturer.

Here's a huge tip:
When you're looking for a manufacturer the easiest and the simplest way to do it is to find a manufacturer that's already manufacturing what you're trying to make.

The easy way to do that is go to Google and type in private label plus whatever it is that you're trying to make.

When I began my search I typed in "private label lip gloss or lip balm". It led me to a website where they were making lip gloss or lip balm already and it was at an affordable price. It was at a price that we could still make her lip gloss affordable for everyone. The plan was to keep it affordable so she would make more sales.

A lot of people, especially family, were asking the same question. What was going to be special or unique and different about Lovie Lip Gloss vs. somebody else's? I told them in the beginning that the difference was not going be in the flavors , I told them that the people were going to be buying a piece of this pretty little girl. It wasn't so much about the lip gloss; I knew that people would buy a piece of this pretty little girl, who had her own business at four years old. She was going to be the face of the company.

Her business started, we found the manufacturer, we began manufacturing her product and we got our first order in January or February, don't remember the exact date.

Our first order was for Cherry Punch. I remember the day Alove got the first order in the mail and it had her picture on it - she was just so excited and I was just excited to see something manifest from an idea to physically hold the product in our hand with her picture on it.

It was amazing!

Each month we came out with a new flavor. It has been doing very well and just like I said in the beginning, Lovie is the face of the company and often times she is the one to sell her lip gloss. And you can't imagine someone turning down a 4yr old who has her own lip gloss.

Here's another quick tip about business that I told her: When she began to get more than one flavor and they would ask how much is her lip gloss? And she'll say you can get one of them for $2 but you can get both flavors for $4. I automatically began to teach her to upsell. Think about that, if you can get two flavors for $4 and you got a $5 bill, often times they'd tell her to keep the extra dollar.

We would get what we really wanted to sell the lip gloss for which was $2.50 but we made it an even $2 to make it simple and easy.

Lovielipgloss is produced in 5 different flavors and she's doing great. She sells her lip gloss where ever she goes; she makes more sales in person than she does from her website because like I said, who could say no to a pretty little girl.

How Shark Tank Came Into Play....

Now let's transition into the submission process to "Shark Tank". I had been on this role of listening to my spirit inside me. I mean, I don't know if you're spiritual reading this but, you can call it what you want. But I call it, my heavenly father, I call it God, the word of God, I call it His spirit speaking to me.

I got on this role of listening to whatever he tells me to do, doing it. And one Sunday evening after church, I was getting ready to watch Sunday night football and it kept tugging on my heart. You need to submit Lovie Lip Gloss to Shark Tank. So I went to Shark Tank's website and it says submit your application via email. I copied and pasted the email into my yahoo account. I knew that since this was going to be an email I had to do something to stand out to get their attention for them to even open the email. So in the email subject line I put **"Pick This Pretty Little Girl"**.

Sticking to my original concept was that Lovie is going to be the seller of the business people are going to buy into her. So I put in the subject line "Pick This Pretty Little Girl". The email ended up being maybe three lines. It said, "Hi I'm Kelly Cole, I'm 31yrs old and my daughter Alove Cole, who is 4yrs old, has her own lip gloss line. Here's her website lovielipgloss.com, looking forward to your reply". I put my name, phone number and my email address for them to contact me.

Now that was Sunday, by Friday the producer from Shark Tank called me. Here's the thing, it was a 310 area code so I automatically knew it was California. I almost did not answer the phone but my spirit told me to answer the phone. I answered the phone and it was the producer from Shark Tank and she was so excited about Lovie's product, and about what she saw on her website, her video and everything. She was just so excited and she wanted it to be on the show.

So I'm like ok great, what's the next step? She said I'm going to send you a package via email. It's a contract; you need to print the contract out. You need to make sure you sign every bit of the contract, read it over answer all questions and we also need a video. I said so in the packet it's going to give you the instructions about the video. Basically, they wanted somebody to it interview style so that the person behind the camera they wanted them to ask you a series of questions.

Here's what we did. My wife, Lovie and I we sat down and answered all the questions in the packet. The contract ended up being about 40 or 50 pages of stuff we had to read sign and answer questions. We filled out the contract and we sat down and we recorded the actual video. We recorded the video and I wanted to show Alove's personality, so Alove and I sat there as my wife asked her the questions, pretty much what ever came to Alove's mind and whatever came to my mind we answered the questions.

The producer said she needed it on her desk by Wednesday so I shot it on Sunday, sent it out Monday through Broadway express. A week goes by and we hadn't heard anything. Two weeks go by and we still didn't hear anything, so I sent the producer an email. I said "hey, I just wanted to make sure you received the package and what's the next step?" No reply. Waited another week, sent her another email, "Hey, I haven't heard anything from you, just wanted to make sure you received the package."

She sent me an email back and said that all of the contestants have been picked for this season and feel free to resubmit of there's a next season.

I wasn't really disappointed because I knew I was writing this book and I knew things work out for a reason. So I didn't' know if it would be a conflict of interest that I'm writing this book and me being on the show. But I do think it was a great thing that I went through the process of submitting a business to Shark Tank.

All in all what I'm trying to tell you is that you want to stand out. When you're doing anything, when you're trying to get picked for something, you want to stand out; you want your uniqueness to shine.

So in the subject line I didn't do the boring subject line, "shark tank audition or Shark Tank application" I put something out of the box. Probably something somebody else didn't even think about - "Pick this Pretty Little Girl".

Now ultimately we did not get on the show but we did make it to the next level. We made it to phase two. We got a lot further than a lot of people. Who number 1 never submitted an application and number two didn't do anything to stand out. So I was very excited about that and to have this experience to share with you in this book. I'm also going to put a copy of the screen shot of the actual email that I sent them. Just so you can see how well it stood out from what I would think the average person will write as an application to audition for shark tank.

Email I Sent To Shark Tank

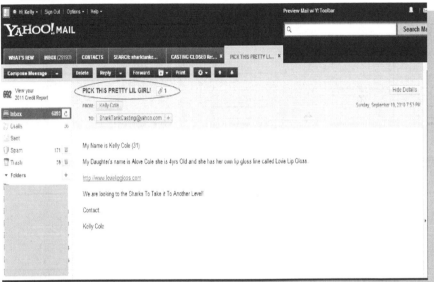

> ### Shark Quote:
> "Every now in then in your life as you try and chase your dream you get to a crossroad where you have to make a decision, which way are you going to go?"
> – Robert Herjavec

My Daughter Alove Cole: www.LovieLipGloss.com

Starting a Business

When I Interviewed Daymond John, he said something very profound to me and I agree with this statement 100%. Daymond said, "When starting a business or any type of entrepreneur endeavor you have to start with what you love". The reason I agree with this 100% is that if you love something, it's going to be that much easier to get up and to do it every day.

Like me, when I wake up in the morning, I cannot wait to get started, get on the computer and check my emails to see what money I made while I was asleep. I can't wait to get involved in my business.

The first time I knew that internet marketing was for me and what I was put here on earth to do, was on a Sunday afternoon I was in Books A Million with my family and I came across this magazine called 'Millionaire Blueprint's. On the cover a guy named Yanik Silver was in a convertible and the caption read 'Web Made Millionaire'. I began to read his story about how he was creating these websites that made income while he slept. He talked about eBooks and different types of services where the customer pays for the product then they're taken to a page to download the product that they've paid for. There was no shipping involved, no heavy lifting, nothing. You create a product once and get paid over and over again.

And it was like the heavens opened up, you heard the musical sounds playing, and I said - this is it, this is what I was put here on earth to do. My love and passion for it just grew more and more as I read about his story and all the other internet marketers as I got deeper and deeper into it.

I remember getting invited to my first internet marketing seminar in Atlanta. I didn't even have money to pay for a hotel. I barely even had money to get there. But I said I was going even if I had to sleep in my car. I had to go because all of the people I was reading about and watching on YouTube were going to be there and that was my opportunity to see them live in the flesh and for free.

When I went to this conference, some of the speakers that spoke…..Matt Bacak, Jermaine Griggs, Joel Comm, Willie Crawford, Ray Edwards ….. All of which are internet marketing gurus / millionaires. I wish I can put it into words how I felt, but I did not want to come home. I didn't even want to leave the conference room. It was a three day conference and for all three days I was probably the first one there in the morning and the last one to leave.

I met a bunch of great people there. A lot of them are still my friends today. Half of the time I didn't even want to leave to get something to eat during the hour lunch break. I would sit there writing notes, thinking of all these ideas and strategies that I was learning. I just knew it was my passion. I didn't want to do anything else.

Now finding my passion didn't come easily. I want to let you know that I tried numerous things to try to make money before I found my actual passion. I was a barber for 10yrs, I used to video weddings, I used to take pictures at weddings, I used to own two clothing stores, a restaurant and I used to and still do event promotions and I still love doing that. I used to do so many different things till I found what I was put here on earth to do.

Getting back to the point, whatever you are going to do, do something you love. Don't do stuff for money. The reason I said that is that all those things I listed before I started internet marketing, I did them for money and as you see now I don't do any of them right now. None of them lasted because when it got down to it, the money wasn't worth the aggravation of actually doing the job because it wasn't something I loved.

Now after I found internet marketing, people were still calling me to record their wedding and most of the time I did it because they were friends or friends of friends. I really did it for the money and because of the relationship. What I found out was, while I was there videoing their wedding, I was thinking about how I could be spending that time making some money on the internet versus holding a video camera. So my mind and focus was never on it especially after I found my passion. The money didn't matter; it was just being able to be engulfed in what I actually enjoyed doing.

When you do things for money, you will make decisions for the wrong reasons because you're under pressure. Because I had no pressure in doing what I love, I made correct decisions.

When Starting A Business or Implementing A New Idea – Act Quickly Says Barbara Corcoran!

Me: Now when it comes to ideas and jumping on things, how important is it to implement things fast?

BC: It's everything, you know what I mean? It's everything. Because I have found, whether you have a tiny business or a big business, if you don't jump on something right away, it's like a bird flying by – it flies off. You get involved in something else, and something *seems* more pressing, you know, because it's in your face, and you have to contend with it – you have to find fire, you have to, you know, deal with a client – you have to deal with what's being thrown at you. So, actually, I always think if I have an idea, I *immediately* move on it. Now, that doesn't mean that every idea is a good idea, but to start an idea is not expensive. To follow it through is expensive sometimes, if you have to put money behind it. But to start that fire and get it burning immediately, it's everything. But I have found, even with myself – and I am a mover, like I like to move on things quick, you know? But even though I have that trait in me, when I don't move immediately on something in my head, it's gone. And it's not that I'm senile, it's just that - life moves on, you know. It's such a fast paced life, and you don't get a chance to do it again. So I see any new idea as immediately very urgent, and it goes to the top of my list. Whereas most people on ideas are tomorrow's business and they allow it to sit, you know, on the bottom of their list or no list at all until they have the time. And you know what, if you try five ideas, and you're going to get one that's a winner. You can guarantee it! But if you're going to get five ideas and move on one, you've got to now have twenty-five new ideas to get a winner. You know, because the odds are stacked against you. So I just believe in moving right out on an idea.

Me: Wow. That's great stuff. It took me a while to get that. I went to an Internet marketing conference with a guy named Mike Litman, He gave me this quote and it changed my life, he said, "You don't have to get it right, you just got to get it going."

BC: Oh, that's a great one!

Me: Yeah, that completely released me to just start getting stuff done rather than waiting on it to be perfect.

BC: Wow, that's a great line. If you don't mind, I'm stealing it and making it my own. You have to erase his name from your memory. You're going to say, "I got this great line from Barbara Corcoran one time." (Laughs)

And that's another point – ideas don't have to be your own. I mean, I don't think I've had an original idea in my life. All I did was go around, see things, and think, "How can I apply *that* good thing to my business?" You know? "What's my version of that business idea?" You know? So, Like for example I remember I got a new design on my website, and I remember I was on my way to London for a vacation – and I hadn't been on vacation in *so long* - and I was on my way to London and I saw an Italian airline board in London putting the flights. And the flights were in color, you know? They put green, blue, yellow, green, blue, yellow, and you could find your flight really easily. And so I *immediately* got to a phone, called back to the States, and told my marketing person at the time and I said, "Here's how I'm going to solve the web problem." I said, "Just put colored bars across the screen to divide up the listings." And you know what? We, all of the sudden, the design on that site was so smart, so easy to read – I mean, not, that's not an idea that gives you a million dollars right away, but it's the accumulation of all these ideas you can get from wherever you go and whatever you do – and I always found out the best ideas I *always* got when I was playing. I *never* had a single good idea at my desk. I never did! I had to go out, and that's when my ideas started to flow.

Me: That is very powerful. I found, when I'm by myself, anywhere, I always pay attention to what's going on – marketing, or how people are doing things. Like you, I get a lot of ideas when I'm out – my phone is filled up, I can't even put anymore notes in it.

BC: (laughs) You're going to have to get one of those new Apple iPads, my husband just got one, you know, it holds a lot more ideas, (laughs), and my husband never gets an idea, so he doesn't need the damn thing, he should give it to me. (laughs)

Me: (Laughs) so you're husband's not an entrepreneur?

BC: He was an entrepreneur, but the minute he married me, he retired. (laughs) I didn't see that train coming! (laughs)

Me: (Laughs) that's funny. So, if you had to start all over, what type of business would you start right now?

BC: Oh gee, that's a good question, because I'm so involved in the business I have, uh that, because I have so many types of businesses now, I'm pretty satisfied, you know, like an overfed dog, in a way. Uh, but if I just had to start over, if I had nothing going on in my life, it would *definitely* be something in the marketing area: advertising, publicity, promotion. You know something in that area. Because that's really what I do well, you know? You can't do everything well, I know I'm very, very good in that arena. So, you certainly always want to go into something you're pretty good at. (laughs) I *certainly* wouldn't be an attorney or an accountant, believe me. That couldn't be less like me, yeah.

Key Point From Barbara:

"If you try five ideas, and you're going to get one that's a winner. You can guarantee it! But if you're going to get five ideas and move on one, you've got to now have twenty-five new ideas to get a winner."

Starting Out Don't Be Afraid To Make Mistakes Says Daymond John

Me: So when you started FUBU and you mortgaged your house, did you have a plan for what you were going to do with the money? Or was it trial and error?

DJ: Oh, it was totally trial and error, and I blew all the money. So, the plan obviously wasn't that great.

Me: So what did you do? What can you share about that? I wouldn't say it's a failure because you learned from it, but what could you share about that experience?

DJ: I share that, and I always tell people this, that the only thing more expensive than an education is ignorance, and the fact that I was ignorant too in making a lot of mistakes that I see a lot of other entrepreneurs make, you know? And I wouldn't say that I wouldn't recommend it to anybody else — they have to go educate themselves. What I should have done was intern in some place or taken up and had some more knowledge, acquired some more knowledge somewhere about the fashion industry and how it works.

And that could have been a gift and a curse, because then I guess maybe I could've, um, wouldn't have taken the same chances if I knew what I knew then — but then I'd be in the same position. But I made a lot of mistakes, a lot. And, you know, I still make mistakes.

Me: Right. So how important is it that you'd recommend to other entrepreneurs, that you go and try things *to* make mistakes, not be afraid to make mistakes?

DJ: Yes, I totally agree, and you always want to make mistakes when you're smaller so you don't make the same mistakes when you're bigger and there's more to risk. But you still have to educate yourself and you still have to take it one step at a time, and don't get emotionally involved in the product — over-emotionally involved in the product — and you're not thinking about business. You know some people really only say, "Well, I have a great idea and the whole world must love it." And that's not necessarily the truth, because the whole world has a price they're willing to pay. And if you can't hit that price, then you have to restructure the business, you know?

Me: That's true. So how do you know when it's time to maybe go in another direction in your business? Say something isn't working and you keep banging your head against the wall — how do you know when it's time to go in another direction?

DJ: Well, when all resources have failed, there's always going to be times for a new direction. But, you know, the good thing is we live in a — world of social media is so good because, you know, that's your report card, you know, at the end of the day. If you have a product and you're putting it out there in the world on websites and things of that nature, and people aren't buying it – people don't know you or don't have any need to buy your product – you have to reevaluate it. You know? You either have to improve the product, reduce the price, or you have to think of other ways to get it out there or other angles to market it, you know?

Me: Right. And still, if nobody buys it, do you recommend quitting that business and going into something else?

DJ: Well, I recommend resetting, you know, really thinking it out, going maybe, you know - if you put some years into this business, you know, you've got to go and get a consultant, look at another company that's doing the exact same product you do. And if you really find that nothing else is working, then yes, you know, you make have to take a breather, step back, then come back to fight another day, you know?

Me: Right. So, what is the proper way to take a product to the market? Like, what is the first thing you do when you receive a product – you know, other than clothing or fashion?

DJ: You mean me, or somebody else?

Well, yourself. Like, what would you do?

DJ: I'm trying to get clarity here; you're saying if I get a product or if I work with an entrepreneur and acquired a product?

Me: Well if you worked with an entrepreneur. Like if you came across a product, and say it's a new product, it hasn't even hit the market yet, what would be your first step to take that product to the market?

DJ: Well the first step is doing due diligence on the product and the entrepreneur themselves, make sure that in the event we do take it to market, all bases are covered. That means that, you know, all trademarks and patents have been registered, nationally and potentially globally, meaning that the company doesn't have any form of debt that can be, you know, put on us. Making sure that insurance is in place. That's the first step — all the preparation behind the scenes, knowing the name is locked in, the URL is locked in, because a lot of people think the name, just because it's theirs and they named it after their child, that all of the sudden that name is theirs. So I would be naming my children Ralph Lauren and Tommy Hilfiger if that was the case. That would be that easy.

Me: Right.

DJ: So you have to know that you have all the names. And then you start bringing the product to market, testing it and, um, the best way — the easiest way is having a website and putting it out on the site and seeing if we can sell it. Then coupling up or partnering up with a distributor, if the distributor is not myself — it could potentially be a company that does something very similar to me. But think about it — if it's food, I don't know how to distribute food, I distribute apparel. So if its food and its perishable, I would have to try to strategically work with a distribution house that understands and has refrigeration and stuff like that, you know? And once it starts getting some legs, you know you just keep growing the business from that point on, you know?

Shark Quote

"When you have the right product, with the right person any one can succeed" – Barbara Corcoran

---

Building A Business

The best way before you get too deep into a business or into a product is to test it out. Now, one of the tips Daymond gave for testing out a new business or a new product is through social media, which I think is great since I am a full time internet marketer. So one of the things he said do is to roll your product out into social media. Test it out. Send it to your Facebook friends & fans, or your Twitter followers. Make some videos about it. Just put it out there and get feedback, see what they think about it. This tip alone could save u millions of dollars. Why invest all this money into something nobody wants, think about it.

Another thing I started out doing when I wanted to test information products was to sell them on eBay, A lot of times it worked out great to let me know if a product is good enough to roll out.

You can also do joint ventures or affiliate programs. Now a joint venture is when you partner with a company or business owner and have them refer your product to their customers or clients. So how you would do that is find someone with a product in a similar niche as you, contact them and ask them if they would be interested in doing a joint venture with you. Another great thing is having an affiliate program where people would share your product with their Facebook friends or Twitter followers that they could make a commission on sales that's made. So start with testing your product through social media and any other medium you have. Remember what Barbara said, "If you have five ideas and you act on all five one of them is guaranteed is to be a winner." So one of the best things to do is to jump on it!

Here are some more Ideas on how you can actually build your business from Daymond and Barbara. The first thing was you can establish your brand through product placement and celebrity endorsements said Daymond. You can do brand integration into TV. That can include reality shows, music videos; they are both powerful because people get to see the product in a lifestyle format. Let's just say on Jersey Shore people want to know what hair gel the Situation is using to get his hair to look like that. If they can see your product in a lifestyle format on that reality shows that makes it desirable. Music videos are great because young kids want to wear what the entertainers are wearing, do what they are doing. So if they can see your product placed inside the music video that can be very profitable to your business.

A great thing you can do is to start making your own music videos and post them on YouTube. Do spoofs of shows and episode, and other music videos and songs. I've done it and it's created a lot of buzz around my business and who I am. I've remade two of Soldier Boy's songs and videos as spoofs just to send traffic to my website and to draw attention to my brand. So I do recommend you doing that, it works!

Once you get going with some television or a viral video campaign you can then follow up your efforts with web marketing and print. The purpose of that is so the consumer sees your product and business in multiple places. This heightens their desire to have that product. So it's almost like this: If I am seeing you everywhere, I see you in music videos, reality shows, in my favorite magazine, in a commercial, online, if I see you all over eventually that is going to create a desire for that product especially if it is endorsed by a celebrity.

A celebrity endorsement could ultimately make your company just as it did for Daymond. It helps if you have a relationship with a celebrity; one of the things Daymond shared with me is that he had sort of a relationship with LL Cool J. When LL decided to start wearing FUBU, Daymond and LL weren't the best of friends, but they were in the same neighborhood. Daymond jokes and says he stalked LL until LL said yes and began to wear his clothing on the road and on his TV shows. One of the best gorilla marketing tactics I have ever seen was when LL Cool J did a GAP commercial but he had on a FUBU hat in the commercial. That was gorilla! Here was FUBU getting all this brand recognition along with the celebrity endorsement, in a multimillion dollar commercial that they didn't have to pay a dime for because their celebrity endorser wore their hat in the commercial. Daymond also shared that a lot of people got fired from the GAP once they figured out what had been done, but it was too late. The video was already all over the airwaves, already on national TV; anywhere you looked they were playing that commercial.

That is why you see people who pose in pictures with celebrities and they will have the celebrity hold their book or their product. There is strategy in that because it is a transfer of power. It is saying that "Hey I'm standing with this person and I'm holding their product, which means I endorse it. Even if I don't' say go buy this product."

[Smart Tip] The power of media or getting press, Often times people believe what they see on TV, what they read in the newspaper, what they see in the magazine. Let's just say you made it to the Today Show, people relate to Today show with honesty, they wouldn't put anybody on there or any product on there that wasn't effective or if they did not endorse it. So it's a transfer of power when your customers see you in different media / press outlets.

Another key point to building your business and establishing your brand is leveraging your relationships that you have with someone close to who you want to connect with. They say that there is six degrees of separation from somebody famous, a celebrity, or someone you want to get in touch with. A great example is when I wanted to interview Daymond. I had just finished up my interview with Barbara and asked Barbara if she would help me (because I watched the show a lot, I could tell the relationship that Barbara and Daymond had versus Barbara and some of the other sharks, another thing I paid attention to was on Facebook I saw a picture of Daymond and Barbara in his office in New York watching the premiere of Shark Tank. That let me know that out of all the sharks Daymond and Barbara were the ones hanging out, which let me know they had a relationship. Based on my interview with Barbara I had a relationship with Barbara so I knew Barbara could introduce me to Daymond. So leverage relationships that you have with somebody close to whom you want to contact. Daymond was my ultimate dream interview, the person that I admired for years. I admired his clothing. I admired him as a business man. So I leveraged my relationship with Barbara to get into contact with Daymond.

> ## "Who Do You Know, That Know Who You Need To Know?" – Author Unknown

Now here's some ways you can hire a celebrity. One of the things you can do is hire them directly. Now I saw this on the Spin Crowd, a reality TV show that comes on E, on this show there is a PR Firm and they get press for people for their products. So what they do is get celebrities to host parties for different products. So one of the products I saw on one of the shows was a sun tanning lotion. So they wanted Mario Lopez to host a party for this sun tan lotion. Now all they wanted to do is associate their name with Mario Lopez and this product even though he didn't flat out endorse the product meaning he didn't do an ad campaign or say "Hey, buy this suntan lotion." If they were able to get media and press around Mario Lopez hosting a party for blank suntan lotion they knew the power in that brand and that celebrity recognition, and that transfer of power of Mario Lopez. Mario Lopez never said that he wore it, never said go out and buy this, never said anything about the product, it's just that fact of him connecting himself with that brand by hosting an event for them. So that is one idea that you can take and use in your business.

That is why you see a lot of reality stars and a lot of celebrities get paid all this money to host party at night clubs, because they are ultimately are the drawer to get the people to come to the party. Why wouldn't these young people come to a party hosted by Kim Kardashian, Bow Wow or a famous athletic star they look up to? People want to be associated with celebrities so they want to be where celebrities are and that makes the club or the promoter a lot of money.

Here's a site that can handle celebrity endorsements for you, celebrity appearances and more. The site is called PrimeTime-Marketing.com. This website can pretty much get any celebrity you want to endorse your product and help you out with the negotiations. You can also contact them through social media; simply ask them for their management or agent's information. Don't just hammer out them a four page letter in their message box; just simply ask them for their management contact information or their agent. Let them know that you have a potential business proposition for them. They will be more than happy to pass on that information versus you trying to conduct business on a social network. A lot of times you can get their management contact information from their website also.

[Gorilla Marketing Tip] Most people like to buy in a crowd even if they have to pay more. In saying that, create frenzies around what you do and your business. Make a lot of noise when you come into the market place. A few ways of doing that is disagree with an expert in that same nature of field or question whether their view or something they had to say is right. Pay attention to current events, make viral videos around current events and what is going on and relate it to your business.

Daymond said "Don't be over emotionally involved in the product that you forget about the business." Know when it is time to restructure the business. This doesn't mean that your product or your business doesn't work; it just means that your approach to the business isn't working. Now after you do that you switch up and you try different things maybe look for another target market for your product. Maybe you're targeting the wrong people, try some different target markets.

When all resources have failed you, it's time to go in another direction. Some of the things you can do are improve the product, change the price, or find other ways to market it. Daymond also said to maybe think about hiring a consultant, someone in the business, or someone who is already doing what you are trying to do. Get a mentor.

The Art Of The Pitch

So how do you prepare to pitch your business in front of shark investors? Whether you're going on shark tank or you're approaching somebody one on one. This is how to prepare.

This is one of the things that Barbara shared, which was the best advice I think I have ever heard, She said "Practice your pitch in front of people you don't know so you will receive the most honest and brutal feedback." She said that most people meet their adversary when they come on Shark Tank or when they are in front of the investor. By the time they get in front of the investors they should be well able to defend their product or service. Defend why it is a good idea and why it will work. She gave the example of asking your mother on how you look or if you are good looking. Your mother is going to lie to you and say you are the most beautiful thing in the world even if you are not. Have them tear your business apart. Get the answers. Be ready to go because the investors are in it just to make money. Mr. Wonderful Kevin O'Leary always said "money has no emotions and he has never cried over money". Money doesn't care; all he cares about when an entrepreneur comes in front of him is how they will make him more money.

5 Things You Much Know Before Pitching Your Business

Five things you must know before you try to pitch your business to an investor.

Number one: You must know your product, you must know your industry, and you must know your competition. What sets you apart from the competition? What is your unique selling proposition? I remember a guy who came on. He had a Lego type product. It was too close and too similar to Legos and he really did not have a unique selling proposition. Pretty much all the sharks passed because he had not done the proper research. I'm sure he knew about his competition, but he didn't know enough, he didn't know they owned most of the market share. There was not enough difference between his product and Lego's. Why would people step away from Lego's to join a new brand?

Number two: You must know your numbers. You must know your Gross. You must have that in your head at all times, which is what you made total. You must know your net profit, how much money you cleared after you paid all expenses. You must know your manufacturer cost. How much of your own money have you put into the business?

Number three: Why is your business worth what you are asking for? I remember a guy his name was Kwame Kuadey that was on the show and he had a gift card re-selling business. They asked him "Why is your business worth what you are asking for?" The first thing he said was because of me number one, what I'm going to put behind the business, and how I am going to drive the business. The potential sales that I see in the future based on what we have already done. That was his answer and they accepted his answer because it was an honest answer.

> **How to evaluate your business properly: You want to times your company three or four times your yearly revenue. So if you did 50,000 dollars then you would estimate your company is worth about 200,000 dollars. Now if you have a patent or something proprietary, that blows everything out the window because someone could see the value based on your not having any competition.**

Number four: Know how you will spend the investors' money. Have a plan. Don't come in and say you are asking for 50,000 dollars and you don't know what you are going to do with the money. Know how you are spending that money, never go in and say it's going to be used for salary or this or that. The type of answers they want to hear is that you are going to use it to boost manufacturing, provide better marketing; you're going to put us in other markets, things like that. Have a plan and know how you will spend their money.

Number five: Know how the investor is going to make their money back. Remember when I said the number one thing they want to know is what is their return on the investment and how they will make their money back. Once again referencing Kevin O'Leary he said "I treat my money like little soldiers and every day I send them out to battle to bring back more prisoners aka to make me more money." So the main thing an investor wants to know is how you will make their money back.

An investor might turn you down just based on the fact that your business is not the type of business they love, or would like to be in. Don't take that personal, find an investor who does love what u do or too greedy to say no to an opportunity to make some money.

Now what are the top 3 things investors look for in a business?

I call them the three P's... Number one: The first P is the **Person**. Barbara and Daymond answered this first. It's all about the person first. Daymond said "There's nothing better than having a great entrepreneur that you won't mind being a partner with." They consider a partnership almost like a marriage. So if your personalities don't come through, if you don't seem genuine, if you don't seem like a person that they would like to be married to, they will pretty much pass on the deal. No matter how good the product is. They both stated that it is about the person, the entrepreneur first. One of the things Barbara shared was that the person has to have that thankful spirit, that entrepreneur drive, that passion. She said nothing makes her feel more warm and fuzzy inside than a partner who is thankful to be working for her. She said that's great motivation for a partner.

The second P is the **Profit**. How much money did you make? How much money has this business made? That's the second P because it's about the money second. Person first, then it's about the money. They want to know how much of a demand it is out there for the product or service that you are presenting to them. That will give them an idea of how far they can take this business.

Third and final P is the actual **Product.** It's always last. One of the things both Sharks stressed was that any product is better if it is proprietary. Whether or not the product is patented and trademarked plays a huge part in the decision. A great patented product will make them salivate. It's almost like smelling blood in the shark tank. It's like they all pounce if they hear that something is proprietary, something has a patent they all salivate over it because it means there is a very limited competition out there and a limited amount of people that can actually jump into that particular niche or category because you own a patent.

That brings me too one of the guys who probably had one of the best pitches on Shark Tank. It was a guy from Soy-Yer Dough. He created a kind of play dough that is gluten free that allowed kids that were allergic to wheat and other chemicals that are in regular play dough to be able to play with play dough. He patented it so no one else could make this type of play dough and began manufacturing this out of his house in his living room. Pretty much all of the sharks wanted a piece of his action because number one it was proprietary it was patented nobody could produce this, and he had play dough and some other toy companies banging on his door to get a piece of his business.

To recap the three P's, Number one the Person, Number two the Profit, and Number three the Product. So make sure you fit in all three of these before you start looking for an investor for your business.

3 P's - Person, Profit & Product

Proper Way To Pitch An Idea

When pitching your idea to a shark investor or an investor you want to potentially invest your business, it's very important to be honest. Don't go into the shark tank or any meeting full of crap because they can smell it a mile away. If you don't know an answer to a question Daymond said it's ok to say I really don't know the answer to this question. I don't know, that's really why I am seeking a partnership of your caliber to help me take this product to the next level. He said that it's acceptable because it is honest. So it's ok to say you don't know certain things. Come prepared as possible to answer the questions. Be thorough in your answers. Answer the questions honestly and answer them to the best of your ability.

It's also very important to know what you want and what you are willing to give. There was a guy on the show who had a golf club idea. His thing was that he was a doctor. What he really wanted was a partner to help take the product to the next level and pretty much make the product. All he wanted was a residual income from the product. He didn't have a passion for the actual product. His main thing was being a doctor, but he had this great idea for a product. So he was willing to give up more than half of his business. He was happy to just receive a residual or a royalty for his product being on the market, which was cool. It was others who came on the show who didn't want to give up half or over half of their business. The product was a part of them; it was something they wanted to work in.

Know the figure you are willing to give up and the percentage of your company. So just say if you come in and you asking for 100,000 dollars for 30% of the company have another number in the back of your head, a percentage of the company you are willing to give. Say hey the most I am willing to give is 45%. If you get to a crossroad and the only way you can make a deal and a shark says that they got to have 50%, you have to decide right then if it is worth it to you to give up half your company to make more money or staying where you are.

Have high energy when you are presenting or pitching. They want to feel your energy exude from you. They want to feel your passion for your product. They want to feel your passion about your business. I remember a lady on the show who had a shoe business. She came in with this whole presentation with music and she was dancing on the aisle. You could tell she loved what she did. She probably had one of the best entrances and high energy of anyone I have ever seen present. Ultimately she didn't get a deal but her presentation was great.

Look them in the eye. This is something Barbara said and this is something I have been a fan of my whole life. There's a great power in looking someone in the eye. Barbara shared this story about the young lady from Grease Monkey Wipes. Barbara said she had spent too much money that day and she was not going to invest in grease monkey wipes. The young lady looked her in the eyes and said "Barbara if you give me a chance I promise you I will not lose your money. I will make you more money." She said because of her having the integrity to look her in the eye, she made the deal. She believed in her and she did exactly what she said she would do. She said that business has net profited over 90,000 dollars in the first year since they became partner.

When an investor decides to partner with you be sure to have a thankful spirit. Tell your partners you appreciate them. You appreciate them for being an entrepreneur and helping you live the American Dream.

Recap
- Be honest.
- Answer all the questions thoroughly.
- Know what you want and what you are willing to give.
- Have high energy when presenting.
- Look the entrepreneur in the eye. Always look people in the eye not just when you are trying to sell the business. The Good Book says the eyes are the gateway to the soul. You can pretty much tell a person's motive, what they are thinking if you look them in the eyes.
- The last thing is to have a thankful spirit.

What **NOT** To Do

The number one mistake that both Barbara and Daymond said they saw entrepreneurs make is overvaluing their company. They said because of the emotional aspect of the business sometimes entrepreneurs overvalue their businesses based on the money they put in. That's really not important to the investor. They care more about how much profit you made, which is why you should base your evaluation on that.

Here's how to evaluate your business properly. You want to times your company three or four times your yearly revenue. So if you did 50,000 dollars then you would estimate your company is worth about 200,000 dollars. Now if you have a patent or something proprietary like we shared before. That blows everything out the window because someone could see the value based on your not having any competition. Daymond also shared this, "Negotiation is all about the value you see, the value seen in something versus somebody else's sees." I'm going to repeat that one more time, "negotiation is all about the value I see versus the value someone else sees in the company." So you have a patent or something proprietary, an investor could evaluate your company ten times more than your yearly revenue because of the potential of not having competition.

Don't over evaluate your company, know your numbers, and be stern in your negotiation, especially if you have a patent or something proprietary.

Never tell them you don't know anything about the industry. There was a guy who created a different type of soda and he created this soda because in the school system in the town he lived in took out regular soda. He wanted to create something to replace the sodas, but he wanted it to be healthier and great tasting for the students. The sharks asked him why did he choose that industry to get into because there are so many soda companies or drink companies that have failed. He said, "To be honest with you I really don't know anything about the soda industry or a bottling company." They said that is probably the worst thing you could have ever said to us. A lot of them were ready to give him money based on his sales, but because he said he didn't know anything about the industry they all backed out.

Don't take the shark comments personally. It's business. It's not personal. You can become friends after the deal is done. Just know this, if you've studied this show Shark Tank, if you've studied Donald Trump's Apprentice you know that it's business. It's nothing personal when they say things or poke at you or they are brutally honest with you about your business. It's not personal. When money is involved or you are doing business, its business and that is what it is. You become friends after the deal is done. Don't think that they hate your guts or they don't like you. It's not even about that. If you notice the sharks a lot of the times get into it themselves, they've all said mean things to each other, but nobody storms off the set, nobody not talks to each other. They realize its business. Now do they go fishing with each other or to the mall or shopping, I'm sure not all of them do that from time to time, but at the end of the day they all realize they are on that show. They are in that boardroom.

They are in there to conduct business. This quote came from a guy named Johan Mach, owner of an internet marketing company and he said this, "Listen business is war, Business is not a game." Now if you treat business like a game, how do you play a game? You play a game to win. You are going to use every strategy, you are going to use every technique you have, you are going to use your best gun, and you are going to win. You are not going out there to pat somebody on the butt. If you are friends you are friends after the game, not during the game. Now in that boardroom, in that shark tank, in that business deal you become friends after the deal is done. So don't' take things personally. Don't' take the comments personally. Don't take the things that they say as if they are attacking your business; know it's all about business. They have to be strong, they have to be stern. You are coming in there, you asking for 250,000 dollars for 10% of your business don't' think it's going to be a patty cake. They want to know and they want to discern you. They want to know what you are going to do with this money and why you have the guts to even walk in there to ask them for their money.

Don't be afraid to ask investors for their money. This comes from Barbara. She says number one: be clear and know what you want. Have a clear plan. Have something written out. Have your idea down. Have your T's crossed and your I's dotted. The key to approaching them is showing them this is how I am going to make you some money. A lot of rich people have money, but they don't have a lot of time. So they do want their soldiers, their money, to go out and produce them money. They really don't have time to search out these deals to invest in, so it's cool for you to approach them, just be clear on what you have and how you are going to make them some money and approach them.

Shark Quote

No Sales / No Orders = No Business
– Kevin O'Leary

Conversation With Barbara Corcoran

Hello?

Thank you so much for coming, Barbara.

BC: You're welcome!

You wanted to just jump right into it?

BC: Yeah, why not? No time like the present, right?

Right, Well first off, let us say thank you so much for doing this interview-

BC: And thank you for being so cooperative with moving around, Gail told me she moved you around a few times, I'm sorry about that.

No problem, it's just an honor to have you on here, so. I was going to do anything to make it happen.

BC: (laughs) Ok good, well you made me happy, so thank you.

(laughs) Alright um, first off, congratulations on the new season of Shark Tank.

BC: Oh, I'm so happy over it, yep I'm so happy for that.

That's great. Alright, well the first question I had, um, was what are the top three things you look for before you consider investing in the business?

BC: Oh, always the same thing – high energy. I just look at the entrepreneur, not so much the business. I focus on the entrepreneur. I look for high energy. I look for thoroughness, not so much in their presentation but in their answers, If trust their answers, you know because people can practice and put on a good show, but it's harder to practice answers that you don't know are going to come at you, you know what I mean? Questions are going to come at you. And then the last thing I always look for is thankfulness. I don't wanna get in bed with my entrepreneur who doesn't have the thankful gene, you know, because it winds up being a miserable marriage.

Gotcha (laughs) so you invest more in the person; it has less to do with the business and more so the person?

BC: Oh, well you know the business has to make common sense. I see many, many businesses that make common sense but I just don't believe that the person who's standing there in front of us, who's going to bring us through the finish line. you could have the best business idea in the world and I won't touch it if I don't think the person standing in front of me can be a star, you know?

Got it.

BC: You know what else too, by the way? You know what else I'm thinking? I've even invested in one or two businesses where, once we got into it, we actually changed the plans so dramatically that it was almost a different business. And I don't care about that, as long as the entrepreneur who's running the show is capable.

Which brings me to the Grease Monkey Wipes, Is that why you invested in that business?

BC: Grease Monkey Wipes is a funny thing. Grease Monkey Wipes is the last presentation we heard after ten days of presentations. That was the closing act for all the sharks, and we had already heard about 200 presentations. I was bleary-eyed, exhausted, and I had gotten onto the set right after the break. I had spent too much money – much, too much money of my own money, much more than I had expected to spend – and I just sat there repeating to myself, "Don't buy anything, don't buy anything, don't buy anything." (laughs) That's all I was saying! So that I wouldn't buy anything. And I didn't buy Grease Monkey Wipes, but when Robert Herjavec went in for twenty-five percent of it, I was so jealous, I couldn't help myself and I just jumped in and said, "Wait right there!" You know, the deal was closing and they were saying, "Yes," and – "Whoa, whoa, whoa, wait right there!" (laughs) And I said, "I'm just so afraid of losing money!" I was honest, because I had just put so much money on the table. And Erin, the female partner of the two, came right up to me and looked me straight in the eye and said, "Please, please, I won't lose your money." And I totally trusted her, I believed her. And she hasn't - they made a $90,000 profit at the end of their first year! (laughs) So, I was so happy, I jumped back in, you know? But, I wasn't planning on doing that. I was surprised my own mouth was talking, honestly. (laughs)

She was really passionate; I really enjoyed her energy, too. She won over a lot of people.

BC: Oh, she won over a lot of people. And you know what? It's such a great power in someone who can look you in the eye. I mean, she just looked you right in the eye, and you almost felt embarrassed for looking away, you know? And she had that, as a partner, she and her partner – his name, uh – it escapes me, God I talked to them last – well, whatever his name is, I'm thinking Ken but it's not. Because she kind of looks like a Barbie doll, he looks like a Ken doll, don't you think? But anyway, (laughs) she had thanked me a hundred times – a hundred times a month! – She says, "Oh, thank you, thank you so much!" Do you know, that's a great motivator for a business partner! Its like, "Oh, I'm appreciated!" Who doesn't like to be appreciated? (laughs)

What is the number one mistake you see entrepreneurs make when they come onto the show to pitch their ideas?

BC: Um, I think almost all of them prepare, but I think none of them practice in front of someone who doesn't like them. And I think that's the best practice in the world. If you practice in front of someone – not your mother, not your dad, not your best friend, not your sister – but practice with someone who really doesn't care for you? They'll *tear your presentation apart*. Because they don't like you, and that's exactly what you need. You really need an adversary on the other side of the table — yet most entrepreneurs walk into the shark tank and they meet their adversaries for the first time. And it shouldn't be! They should be very comfortable having someone challenge them and poke around and make them feel diminished, to some degree, and they need to defend their product.

Wow, that's very powerful, I've never thought about that. That's a great way to get honest feedback too, isn't it?

BC: Oh, you get honest feedback, definitely. You ask your mother how handsome you are and she's only going to lie to you and tell you, "Amazing!" (laughs)

(laughs) Always momma's baby, no matter what!

BC: Every momma's baby makes a good husband, that's my opinion. (laughs) And my sixteen-year-old, six feet tall, he's my little baby! (laughs) And somebody's going to get lucky getting him, he better pick out somebody good or I'm going to kill her. (laughs)

Does he play sports?

BC: Oh. Yeah, he lives for sports. I mean, he's a good student because he has to be, but he lives for sports. He loves them. Lacrosse is his number one, and second is swimming. And he only does the swimming to get in shape for lacrosse, I think.

So you say he has to be a good student?

BC: He has to be a good student, of course! He's a smart kid, I mean – can I tell you the truth? If he wasn't a smart kid, you know, didn't have brains, he wouldn't have to be a good student, in my opinion. It's fine, it's just – do your best. But if he's got really big brains in his head, he's got to be a good student, or it's a waste! God should've given it to somebody else if he's not going to use it. So he's under a lot of pressure to be a good student. I never say, "Get A's, get B's," I don't do any of that. I just say, "Hey, are you really trying your best?" I mean, you try your best at anything, you're going to succeed. That's what I think. So, it's more of getting in the habit of doing your best than trying to get good grades.

That's great. So what was it about school – I saw your Facebook, you put you got straight D's in high school – what was it about high school that you got D's?

BC: Well, I wanted to continue my perfect record from grammar school, which was straight D's. I didn't want to have to get to know any other letters in the alphabet – I knew the D's, and when it was on that report card, I felt very comfortable. So I had it in grammar school and high school and I continued to get them in college. How I got into college was nothing short of a miracle, because they opened a small girl's college, a half-hour from my home, that was actually a nunnery – you know, they made these nun's, the habits, the little white things and the black veils. But, they didn't have enough nuns coming in so they decided to open it up to other girls – and thank God for that or I would've never gone to college, I would've never gotten in. So I had D's all the time. But you know what the truth is? The fact of the matter is I was like ten percent of the population, because I was dyslexic. And in those days, they didn't have a label for it, they just though you were stupid. There wasn't any kind of, you know, ways to teach, you know. Multi-sensory teaching methods – I mean, you sat in class and you learned with the other fifty kids in the school. Their way, you know? So I just couldn't read, that's all, I couldn't read. And if you can't read, you can't do anything, that's the truth. But you know what, I had more, than anyone in my class or maybe the school, more daydreams. And you wanna know, I was *great* at dreaming up an idea. And you wanna know, that's what made me my money. It wasn't being good at math – I still can't read a financial statement, I don't worry about it. I figure, the business is doing well, it's going to make money, and that's all you really have to focus on. But, I really learned how to daydream. I mean, I could think of an idea quicker than a wink, and I attribute that to all those years in that jailhouse everybody else calls "school". I got the hell out of there, and I was free to actually, you know, daydream and do what I wanted! You know? It was great getting out of school.

Wow. That's awesome, I totally agree with that. Now when it comes to ideas and jumping on things, how important is it to implement things fast?

BC: It's everything. Do you know what I mean? It's everything. Because I have found, whether you have a tiny business or a big business, if you don't jump on something right away, it's like a bird flying by – it flies off. You get involved in something else, and something *seems* more pressing, you know, because it's in your face, and you have to contend with it – you have to deal with what's being thrown at you. So, actually, I always think if I have an idea, I *immediately* move on it. Now, that doesn't mean that every idea is a good idea, but to start an idea is not expensive. To follow it through is expensive sometimes, if you have to put money behind it. But to start that fire and get it burning immediately, it's everything. But I have found, even with myself – and I am a mover, like I like to move on things quick, you know? But even though I have that trait in me, when I don't move immediately on something in my head, it's gone. And it's not that I'm senile, it's just that - life moves on, you know. It's such a fast paced life, and you don't get a chance to do it again. So I see any new idea as immediately very urgent, and it goes to the top of my list. Whereas most people on ideas are tomorrow's business and they allow it to sit, you know, on the bottom of their list or no list at all until they have the time. And you know what, you try five ideas, and you're going to get one that's a winner. You can guarantee it! But if you're going to get five ideas and move on one, you've got to now have twenty-five new ideas to get a winner. You know, because the odds are stacked against you. So I just believe in moving right out on an idea.

That's great stuff. It took me a while to get that too. I went to an Internet marketing conference with a guy named Mike Litman, you ever heard of him?

BC: Yeah, I think I have heard of him.

This one quote changed my life, he said, "You don't have to get it right, you just got to get it going."

BC: Oh, that's a great one!

Yeah, that completely released me to just start getting stuff done rather than waiting on it to be perfect.

BC: Wow, that's a great line. If you don't mind, I'm stealing it and making it my own. You have to erase his name from your memory. You're going to say, "I got this great line from Barbara Corcoran one time." (laughs)

Will do, will do.

BC: And that's another point – ideas don't have to be your own. I mean, I don't think I've had an original idea in my life. All I did was go around, see things, and think, "How can I apply *that* good thing to my business?" You know? "What's my version of that business idea?" You know? So, Like for example I remember I got the *best* design on my website, and we were online years before my competitors were through just happenstance but I remember I was on my way to

London for a vacation — and I hadn't been on vacation in *so long* - and I was on my way to London and I saw an Italian airline board in London putting the flights. And the flights were in color, you know? They put green, blue, yellow, green, blue, yellow, and you could find your flight really easily. And so I *immediately* got to a phone, called back to the States, and told my marketing person at the time — corporate — and I said, "Here's how I'm going to solve the web problem." I said, "Just put colored bars across the screen to divide up the listings." And you know what? We, all of the sudden, the design on that site was so smart, so easy to read — I mean, not, that's not an idea that gives you a million dollars right away, but it's the accumulation of all these ideas you can steal from wherever you go and whatever you do — and I always found out the best ideas I *always* got when I was playing. I *never* had a single good idea at my desk. I never did! I had to go out, and that's when my ideas start to flow.

I found, when I'm by myself, anywhere, I always pay attention to what's going on — marketing, or how people are doing things. Like you, I get a lot of ideas when I'm out — my phone is filled up, I can't even put anymore notes in it.

BC: (laughs) You're going to have to get one of those new Apple Ipads, my husband just got one, you know, it holds a lot more ideas. Yeah, yeah, that's what you got to do. (laughs)

BC: And my husband never gets an idea, so he doesn't need the damn thing, he should give it to me. (laughs)

(Laughs) So you're husband's not an entrepreneur?

BC: He was an entrepreneur, but the minute he married me, he retired. (laughs) I didn't see that train coming! (laughs)

(Laughs) That is funny. So, if you had to start all over, what type of business would you start right now in this economy?

BC: Oh gee, that's a good question, because I'm so involved in the business I have, uh that, because I have so many types of businesses now, I'm pretty satisfied, you know, like an overfed dog, in a way. Uh, but if I just had, if I had nothing going on in my life, I would *definitely* be something in the marketing area: advertising, publicity, promotion. You know something in that area. Because that's really what I do well, you know? You can't do everything well, I know I'm very, very good in that arena. So, you certainly always want to go into something you're pretty good at. (laughs) I *certainly* wouldn't be an attorney or an accountant, believe me. That couldn't be less like me, yeah.

So the thousand dollars you borrowed to get started, did you borrow that from a bank?

BC: I borrowed it from my boyfriend.

(laughs) So what did you do with the thousand dollars to begin your business?

BC: Well that was easy, I mean, the thousand dollars stretched very far – it was in 1973. So I was able to, with that thousand dollars, buy two ads in the New York Times – two classified ads, which then drove the real estate business in New York, you know. You didn't have the Internet, so everybody found their properties in the New York Times. So it enabled me to buy two three-line ads in the New York Times, okay, twice a week – Saturday and Sunday – for an entire month. And it paid for my telephone, you know, it operated out of my apartment with my two roommates. But I paid for my telephone, which wasn't much – it was twelve dollars a month – plus the ads. And that got me through a whole month. By the second week, I did a rental, I rented something. That's what my business started out as – renting apartments, for quick cash, you know? And so the second week I made $340, and now I had, you know, I didn't quite recoup the cost but I had another two weeks, almost two weeks to stay a business. And I made another rental. So, that's how it kept going on the business – that's how I stretched the money.

So, the ads you posted, they were for somebody else's properties that you rented out? Or were they your property?

BC: Oh no, I didn't have a pot to pee in, never mind a property. No they were definitely landlord properties, you know? Everything was open game, then. In other words - and by the way I was very lucky, it was a very bad real estate market. There were many vacancies in New York. It was on the heels of one of the presidents saying to New York, "Go to hell," when the city was bankrupt – so it was in the worst time. And what was great about that was that landlords needed help. And what's great about bad times is that the old dog has to learn new tricks; and very often they're not able to, so the world is open to newcomers. And so I was so lucky I started in a bad market because people were willing to try anything because everybody had problems. And so my little, you know, my pitch to the landlord, "Give me an apartment, give me an apartment, give me an apartment to rent," they were open to it. Whereas if we had a really good market, they wouldn't have taken my call, you know?

Which leads me to my next question: Is this a great time to get into real estate?

BC: Well, I have a prejudiced eye, because I grew up in a bad market, so I happen to think that's a great advantage, okay? So, I think it's a *great* time to get into real estate – every piece of it – because so many of the, for example, as an agent, as a broker agent, whatever you want to call it, trading property/selling property is a great time because so many of the old dogs are out of business. They've been chewed up and spit out by their time. And so there are empty desks and there's opportunity. You might say it's a bad time to buy, because of the appetite of people to buy is, you know, very questionable. People are scared to buy because the real estate market has been so rocky. But, on the other hand, they're not listening to anybody, even the old agents. So you have a chance to go in there and shake things up. And if you're smart enough and brave enough and have a rich uncle with some cash, you can buy a property and renovate them and flip them, or renovate them and hold them – there couldn't be a better time! We have 4% money financing. So, let's say you bought a $200,000 property, that $200,000 property will have cost you; roughly, I'll say $1800 to pay back the mortgage on $200,000 ten years ago? Right now, of course, you're only $900. So, you can usually buy property or rent it out and make a profit today, in this kind of a market. So it's really a golden opportunity – reduced prices and cheap money at the same time. That usually never happens, you know, you usually have one or the other. So it couldn't be a better time, as an investor. But, you know, you need brass balls – you have to be courageous, because once people like to buy in a crowd when everyone else is buying, even if they have to pay more, they like to see a lot of people around them doing the same thing. This is a lonely kind of time, but that's always when the killers come out and they make their killing.

You say the best thing you need to have is either your own cash or a rich uncle, somebody to invest in you to make that happen?

BC: Yeah, let me tell you something that I learned. I buy property now as investments – I have for the last 15-20 years and then I got a little extra cash, that's what I put my money in, okay? And you know what? I didn't have the time to get to know neighborhoods. So what I have is – I went out and found a partner – a real estate salesman, who I trusted as a partner – to find the property, judge the property, buy the property, and rent the property and manage the property, because I have no time. So think of how beautiful that music is, I mean here's a person who's much likely younger – no money to invest – but they really have the knowledge. They really know their market, you know, they can size things up. So they're the perfect partner for me and I'm the perfect partner for them – you know, I have the cash, they have the knowledge, and together we've done very well on these properties So they become my partner on these properties with no cash, but it's all their responsibility, which I don't have the time for. So now I know that someone's really watching my ass, right? And that's true anywhere in America, wherever you are. There are rich people who love to invest but don't have the time – because when you're rich, you don't have the time, and when you're poor you have the time but you don't have the money. And so these are natural partnerships that are able to be made all over, but people don't see it that way. And I was more aggressive maybe than the typical rich person, and I wanted to cash in on this great wave of appreciation that I saw all around me in New York. But, even if they're not knocking on your door, you can go knocking on theirs if you really know you're market. It's kind of like pitching on "Shark Tank" – "Hey! Let me tell you how I'm going to make you some money! Here's my idea," you know? And so I think the money is available to anybody if they're smart enough to realize that there's no lock on it – it's a matter of selling somebody on giving it to you.

What would you say would be a good return on investment, or percentage? Like say you were approached by somebody to invest, what would you say would be a good percentage or ROI?

BC: That's a funny question because the truth of the matter is I never made any return on any of my investments because that wasn't my goal. My goal was to get in early on an upcoming area – so I got properties in areas of Brooklyn that most people though weren't so good, but I always had my partner – my new partner that really knew it well and knew what was happening. I had bought properties in South Bronx, I bought properties in any area that I thought might be appreciating where I had a good partner who knew it, right? But I never made money on the properties in the first few years because the way I would structure it was – I would just want to put in enough cash where the good deal is. I just wanted to break even – I wanted to plop the cash down, usually 20%, and then I just wanted to break even, I knew I had to put money in every month, you know? And what happens is rents go up, you mortgage stays the same, and what happens is your properties start creeping up in appreciation, and that's where I was after making my money, off the appreciation.

You went out and found a real estate agent; he didn't approach you, right?

BC: No, I went out and I hooked people, definitely. You know why, because most people are too intimidated to approach somebody, and it's a joke! You know? It's a false smokescreen that you created for yourself so you think you can't get it, you know? But everybody has the right to be there. And you can pretty much get into where you want if you have a viable proposition, that's what I think. Maybe not to the first guy, the second guy, the third guy, but hammer away, you know? Like you said, just get it started and sooner or later you'll find yourself in the spot you wanted to be in.

That's it, you don't have to get it right, you just have to get it going.

BC: Yep. (laughs) Remember, remember, I said that. Remember I said that, right? (laughs)

Yes, Barbara told me that. (laughs)

You got to say, "Hey, I was doing this interview with this guy named Kelly Cole and he gave me this wonderful quote, I want you to hear it."

BC: I'll say, "I was doing this interview with this wonderful guy named Kelly, and I told him the best advice he ever wanted to hear, 'You don't have to get it right, you just have to get it going.'" (laughs)

That is great, that is great. So you guys still taking applications for the new season of "Shark Tank"?

BC: Yeah, the best thing to do is, they really are combing through them right now, I don't think that's going to last for so long. Because I even ran into someone who had this wacky opera business in Manhattan, she says, "I just got a call from 'Shark Tank', they want me to come to LA!" So I was like, "Whoa, they really are getting these people up right now." So all you have to do is go to ABC.com and click on "Shark Tank" and you submit your application, it's really easy.

That's it.

Next thing, can you do me a huge favor, Barbara?

BC: Yeah, what's that?

Can you help me get an interview with Daymond?

BC: Daymond? Sure. But this is what you do. Send me a heart-felt, two line or three line email right now and I'll forward it to Daymond before I get on this plane, okay? And let me give you, because I know Daymond and I love Damon more than any of the other sharks, he's truly the most genuine guy in the bunch, you know what I mean? He's genuine through and through, he's a stand-up great guy. So, the most appealing thing to Daymond is to say A) you were talking to me, and I was you second choice for an interview, and you begged me to introduce you to Daymond because he's your hero. Something like that. Okay? And then I'll take your email, and bang, send it over to Daymond – on his personal phone so he'll see it, and include your email and phone number, but let me give you my address to get into my phone, okay? So that I get it, alright?

Thank you so much. But you know what you just told me, that was the truth.

BC: What's the truth? Oh I'm sure it is the truth, because he's deserving of that. You know what I mean? You know what Daymond said to me? The first thing on the set that I laughed my ass off and I so much needed to laugh because I was so scared – I did a terrible, terrible job the first day, and there was another dame they were considering replacing me with, and I was scared to death. So I said to Daymond, "Daymond, you know, I'm doing such a bad job here, I'm sure they're going to axe me. " And he patted me on the shoulder, and you know he's got that great warmth to him? And I hardly knew him, you know? And he patted me on the shoulder and he said, "Don't you worry about a thing, honey, you're the token woman and I'm the token black guy. (laughs) But you wanna know something? I just sat totally relaxed and laughed my ass off, it kind of turned me around. Do you know what I mean? I kind of felt like I had an insurance policy (laughs). So I loved him right then, I said, "I'm in love with this guy." But send that right away, because my flight leaves in 19 minutes and if you send that off to me, I'll send it right to Daymond.

Okay.

BC: But if for some reason it doesn't happen it's because the plane is leaving early, but I don't think it is, it's supposed to leave at twelve.

Thank you so much, Barbara, for doing this. I really appreciate it.

BC: My pleasure, and thanks so much again for being so nice and accommodating me on the time schedule.

Hey it's awesome. I just wanted to make it happen. I 'm just honored you wanted to take this call.

BC: Okay, well thank you so very very much, huh?

No problem and you have a great day!

My Key Takeaways From Barbara Corcoran

The first thing that stuck out to me that Barbara said is her rule of five theory. Her rule of five theory is that if you have five ideas that you act on, you are guaranteed to have at least one winner. She said but if you have five ideas and you only act on one it's going to take 25 ideas before you have that one winner. If you get an idea for something, act on it quickly. One out of five is going to be a winner that's going to produce you some income. So act quickly and move on your ideas fast.

Second take away I got from Barbara was when she said don't be afraid to ask for money. Don't be afraid to approach the people with the money. Just have a clear idea on what you want and how you are going to make them money.

Takeaway 3 - The power of networking. It's something I knew on a smaller scale, but at the end of the interview because I and Barbara felt like a pretty good rapport with each other. At the end of the interview I felt so comfortable that I asked her to introduce me to Daymond to get an interview with him. Now I had been trying to go through the proper resources to get an interview with Daymond, but that just wasn't working. So I leveraged my relationship with Barbara to get an interview. Which I got, and I appreciate that. I learned the power of networking.

Also, one of the cool things that she shared was that she is dyslexic just as I am. In school I didn't know the name for it, but all I knew is that I read words backwards. I saw things backwards and sometimes it hindered how I read. So it was cool to learn that she is dyslexic just like me and a lot of other entrepreneurs. That just goes to show you that you don't have to be the smartest Crayola in the bunch to make a lot of money, to live your dreams, to be successful. So just keep pushing and keep doing what you're doing. It doesn't matter what nobody calls you or what may be standing in your way just go for it.

Takeaway 4 - Be a daydreamer. Be a daydreamer of ideas. It was very refreshing to know that somebody shared in that also. I am a huge daydreamer. I am always thinking of ideas. When I am out and about I am always looking to see how people are marketing things. I look to see what the billboards are saying, what people are wearing. I try to always stay up on the latest trends. I'm always thinking of some greater idea of how I can make even more money.

Takeaway 5- Most people like to buy in a crowd even if they have to pay more. We all know this from experience. It's almost like the story of a guy just stopping in the middle of the street and looks up and before you know it there are three people stopped looking up, then there's four, then there's five, then there's twenty five, then there's fifty, then there's a hundred, then there are three hundred people just standing there looking up and nobody knows what they are looking for. People like to feel a part of the crowd. They like to be included in the "in" crowd or the "A" list like celebrities.

Conversation With Daymond John

DJ: Hello?

Hello? What up, Daymond?

DJ: Hey! What's happening?

How you doing, man?

DJ: I'm good; what's going on?

Not much, man. Thank you so much for doing this interview, man.

DJ: No problem, my pleasure.

Well, first off I wanna say congratulations on your new season of "Shark Tank".

DJ: Oh, thank you. Can you hear me, man?

I can hear you good.

DJ: Okay, good.

So what is the main thing you're looking forward to this season?

DJ: Um, I'm excited about the new guests they're bringing on. You know, they're bringing on Jeff Foxworthy, and Mark

Cuban. So I'm really interested in mixing it up with them, getting into a couple of shark fights, you know? Get it going, and um, you know I'm always excited about meeting the new entrepreneurs, you know, and the new opportunities out there.

Okay. So what are the top three things you look for before you invest in a business?

DJ: Well, generally, it's the person, you know, presenting the business. You know, if the person's going to be still aligned with the business and they're not selling the patent, you know? Because, you know, you're going to be dealing with the partner, and that's someone you'll be talking too often. I think the second thing is, I think the product itself has to have some legs, and you know hopefully it's patented or proprietary and it's a great idea and there's a total upswing on the product. And then third of all, I look for what kind of money, or what kind of revenue, has it generated this year – it shows that there's an actual demand for it out there.

Got you, so most important is the person?

DJ: Yep.

What is the number one mistake you see entrepreneurs make when they come on the show to pitch their idea?

DJ: Overvaluing their company or their idea. You know, somebody may be into a product, you know, they may have put $200,000 - $300,000 into a product, and they believe they should be getting, you know, 2, 3, 4, 500,000 out of the investor when that's not the investor's issue. The investor's issue is: did you sell the product and did you generate revenue.

Right, so what's the proper way to evaluate your business?

DJ: Well, you know that becomes tricky, you know? First of all, that becomes some form of math when you basically times your company 3 or 4 times its annual revenue. So if you did $50,000 you try to say, you know, that your company's worth $200,000. Um, but again, if you do have a proprietary product, or some kind of patent, that can throw everything out of the window because, you know, somebody may feel that the value is worth way more because you don't have any competition on the product.

The patent or the proprietary product, could actually boost the value that you ask for?

DJ: Yes, the value that you ask for or what you expect. Negotiation's all about what value I see in it against the value do you see in it.

It makes a lot of sense. So, what's the proper way – what's a tip you could give somebody who comes to the "sharks" to invest in a business? What's the proper way to pitch an idea to an investor?

DJ: Well, I think the proper way is to have all your answers, and even sometimes your answers may be that, you know, "I'm coming to you because I don't have these answers, and with the money and the funds and the research, I will be able to get you these answers." Don't just come and assume and throw things around, because you're talking to five seasoned investors, you know? We always like to feel like you've done as much research as you can on the product. Um, so that's the first thing. I think also, devaluation, you know? A lot of times, because of the sharks and the format of the show, we can't underbid what you ask for. You need to bid the appropriate amount or we'll have to ask for way more in equity for your product.

I was going to ask why is that, why can't you ask for a different amount that the entrepreneur puts out?

DJ: That's just the rules of the show. You know? That if somebody comes on and they say, "I need a half a million dollars," then we need to start negotiation at a half a million. So the only area they have to negotiate would be, if they say, "I need a half a million for 20% of the company," I may say, "Well, for a half a million – I don't mind the half a million, but I need 75% for the company for that amount of cash."

So the only negotiation there is the percentage they're willing to give up?

DJ: Correct.

So last season you invested in the Soy-Yer Dough. What was it about that business that made you want to invest in it?

DJ: That one was a funny one because I had gotten stabbed in the back in a couple of other joints with, um, Robert and Kevin, and I remember that one I was trying to botch the negotiation for them, even though I did like the product. I was trying to botch the negotiation. But, the proprietary aspect of the product is what made it attractive, gluten free and helpful to kids, so I thought that was a great angle. And I knew that, Kevin had done some sort of deals in the past with Play-doh. So I felt like there was the aspect of getting a great distributor with the product with this great, you know, angle to it.

So, I notice that you all said that he did a great job negotiating. What are some of the things that a new entrepreneur who's coming on to Season Two could use from his presentation?

DJ: From Soy-Yer Dough?

Yeah.

DJ: I don't really recall the aspect of his presentation, you know, the point that made him so good, so I wouldn't be able to give you an accurate answer unless I go back and review it.

Okay, so are there particular types of business that you're looking to invest in at this point in time?

DJ: I'm looking for anything. But the things that are really attractive to me, generally, are items that are not, as we call it, SKU-heavy, you know? They don't have a lot of different items, you know? Because I make clothing, I make apparel, and in one season I can make 3 or 400 different pieces, when you break down size and color and everything else. I like items that are one, two, four piece things that, you know, not heavy inventory. I love items that can be viewed globally. I like items that have obviously had some kind of history of selling good, you know- and not necessarily just to everyday people, but I would really like a record of having it sell to stores, which is always more attractive. And again, patent and proprietary products are best. And it all comes down, also, to a great entrepreneur who I don't mind being a partner with, you know? Some of the entrepreneurs that I have, um, invested in – their product is okay, but I'm starting to trying to do more things with them as a person, and maybe have some more businesses coming up.

That's great, which brings me to one of my other questions: are your original partners, at FUBU, are they partners in any of your other businesses?

DJ: Yeah, they're partners in some of my other businesses.

So when you started FUBU, what was it about fashion that made you want to go into fashion instead of something else? Because I'm sure that you maybe had other ideas. But what was it about fashion that made you go into fashion?

DJ: It was just some of, I'm just a big fan of fashion, I was a fashionable kid, and this new type of fashion, which, for lack of a better term, urban or young men's or whatever the case is, was coming on the scene. It was really attractive to me. So, it was just perfect for me.

I remember a tie top hat that I had; I remember back in the day, I had a blue and white striped one.

DJ: That was from us?

No, this was before – when they first came out, relating to your story, when you start sewing them up. Kind of like a similar thing, I didn't go sell them; I just went all over Chicago looking for one.

DJ: (laughs)

I think I saw Busta Rhymes with one.

DJ: I remember seeing Busta or De La Soul with one.

So are you and your friends, your partners when you started FUBU, are you still close?

DJ: Yeah, very close. They're my brothers.

So what is it about them that make them stay in the background, and you've always been the one that's always in the forefront, even now.

DJ: Um, I mean everybody has a calling. One of them, I mean, they're really not that "in the background", one handles a sufficient amount of models with a modeling agency, besides all of the FUBU and all of the public things we do. The other one's becoming really recognized in fashion as almost a couture expert in a lot of different fashion. He has a blog called "A Fashion Mind" where, you know, people basically come to him as a guru of fashion. And the other one, he's chosen, you know he's always wanted to stay in the background. I think that I, more than the others, have gotten to the forefront of the business by my consulting and my branding and by being an author and writing books of the knowledge of branding and motivational speaking. That's what really put me there.

You really don't see them, you know, you're pretty much everywhere, like you said. You do shows and things like that; you don't see them in too many shows and different things like that. Even your social media presence, like I don't really see them in social media.

DJ: The other one with "A Fashion Mind", J. Alexander, he has just as many follows as I have. Just in his world, you know? His world is really heavy, you know? You wanna know sample sales, or what designer's moving from this company to that company, you know, he has a pretty strong following.

That's good. So when you started FUBU and you mortgaged your house, did you have a plan for what you were going to do with the money? Or was it trial and error?

DJ: Oh, it was totally trial and error, and I blew it, all the money. So, the plan obviously wasn't that great.

So what did you do? What can you share about that? I wouldn't say it's a failure because you learned from it, but what could you share about that experience?

DJ: I share that, and I always tell people this, that the only thing more expensive than an education is ignorance, and the fact that I was ignorant too in making a lot of mistakes that I see a lot of other entrepreneurs make, you know? And I wouldn't say that I wouldn't recommend it to anybody else – they have to go educate themselves. What I should have done was intern in some place or taken up and had some more knowledge, acquired some more knowledge somewhere about the fashion industry and how it works.

And that could have been a gift and a curse, because then I guess maybe I could've, um, wouldn't have taken the same chances if I knew what I knew then – but then I'd be in the same position. But I made a lot of mistakes, a lot. And, you know, I still make mistakes.

Would you recommend to other entrepreneurs to go and try things *to* make mistakes, and not to be afraid to make mistakes?

DJ: Yes, I totally agree, and you always want to make mistakes when you're smaller so you don't make the same mistakes when you're bigger and there's more to risk. But you still have to educate yourself and you still have to take it one step at a time, and don't get emotionally involved in the product – over-emotionally involved in the product – and you're not thinking about business. You know some people really only say, "Well, I have a great idea and the whole world must love it." And that's not necessarily the truth, because the whole world has a price they're willing to pay. And if you can't hit that price, then you have to restructure the business.

That's true, so how do you know when it's time to maybe go in another direction in your business? Say something isn't working and you keep banging your head against the wall – how do you know when it's time to go in another direction?

DJ: Well, when all resources have failed, there's always going to be times for a new direction. But, you know, the good thing is we live in a – this world of social media is so good because, you know, that's your report card, you know, at the end of the day. If you have a product and you're putting it out there in the world on websites and things of that nature, and people aren't buying it – people don't know you or don't have any need to buy your product – you have to reevaluate it. You know? You either have to improve the product, reduce the price, or you have to think of other ways to get it out there or other angles to market it.

Right, And still, if nobody buys it, do you recommend still quitting that business and going into something else?

DJ: Well, I recommend resetting, you know, really thinking it out, - if you put some years into this business, get a consultant, look at another company that's doing the exact same product you do. And if you really find that nothing else is working, then yes, you know, you make have to take a breather, step back, then come back to fight another day.

What is the proper way to take a product to the market? Like, what is the first thing you do when you receive a product –other than clothing or fashion?

DJ: You mean me, or somebody else?

Well, yourself. Like, what would you do?

DJ: I'm trying to get clarity here; you're saying if I get a product or if I work with an entrepreneur and acquired a product?

Well if you worked with an entrepreneur. Like if you came across a product, and say it's a new product, it hasn't even hit the market yet, what would be your first step to take that product to the market?

DJ: Well the first step is doing due diligence on the product and the entrepreneur themselves, make sure that in the event we do take it to market, all bases are covered. That means that, you know, all trademarks and patents have been registered, nationally and potentially globally, meaning that the company doesn't have any form of debt that can be, you know, put on us. Making sure that insurance is in place. That's the first step – all the preparation behind the scenes, knowing the name is locked in, the URL is locked in, because a lot of people think the name, just because it's theirs and they named it after their child, that all of the sudden that name is theirs. So I would be naming my children Ralph Lauren and Tommy Hilfiger if that was the case. That would be that easy.

Right.

DJ: So you have to know that you have all the names. And then you start bringing the product to market, testing it and, um, the best way – the easiest way is having a website and putting it out on the site and seeing if we can sell it. Then coupling up or partnering up with a distributor, if the distributor is not myself – it could potentially be a company that does something very similar to me. But think about it – if it's food, I don't know how to distribute food, I distribute apparel. So if its food and it's perishable, I would have to try to strategically work with a distribution house that understands and has refrigeration and stuff like that.

DJ: And you know, once it starts getting some legs, you know you just keep growing the business from that point on.

What are your favorite forms of marketing? Like, do you prefer TV, print, Internet-base? How would you market that product?

DJ: I prefer brand integration into television, and I do that actually for myself as well as for my other companies. I prefer getting a product and putting it on, a video, a reality show, something of that nature where peoples start to see the product in a lifestyle format and they start to gravitate towards that. That's what, I prefer that initially. Then I would probably follow up with some form of websites or print so people, after they've witnessed it someplace, can say, "Okay, now how do I get it?" And you have to get that information into print or something like that.

Which has worked great for you, right? Remember, you always talk about the Gap commercial that LL wore that FUBU hat in.

DJ: Yep. That was the tipping point for me, actually.

Did you plan that? Or LL, was that his idea?

DJ: LL planned it.

Wow.

DJ: LL, and that's why, you know I love celebrity endorsements, you know? When you get somebody like LL, behind you and he goes hard for you, man, you know – that's a typical example of how it can really make you.

So y'all started out as friends and he took it on, or how did that relationship come about?

DJ: Well LL was a neighborhood friend associate, so I can't say we were the best of friends, and I just kept coming to him with the product, and I used to go to his tours and be like a roadie on his tours, and you know, he was gracious enough to say, "You know what, this product, you know, I'm being looked at by a lot of companies like Nike, Timberland, stuff like that, and if I start wearing this product, I may jeopardize my potential, you know, sponsors." He said, "But I believe in you and I believe in the brand and the product and what you guys are doing, and I'm going to go hard for you." And he decided to.

I remember he had it on *everywhere*. I mean, I remember the Vibe cover, you remember that? Him with all his wife and kids, and he had the red FUBU hoodie with the hat on?

DJ: Trust me, I remember every one of those, baby. (laughs) It was a very important time of my life.

DJ: I said those were very important times of my life and, um, and you know that really gave me – you know, it's the way you're brought up, whether personally or brought up in business, that gives you the outlook. And that gives me my outlook, my excitement with helping these other new entrepreneurs because I was on that - (coughs) Sorry, I was on that receiving end of being somebody who needed that help. So, LL has definitely helped me in my train of thought.

I know exactly what you mean. So, what advice would you give somebody that's, you know, maybe thinking about or wanting to start a clothing line? What advice would you give them?

DJ: Well, I would say that…Well, first of all, I don't care what you're trying to start – a clothing line, or, you know, an ant farm, or whatever it is. I've always told people that the most important thing – and I don't wanna use a whole lot of clichés – but the most important thing ever is to do something you love. And that is very, very important because a lot of people that, money is the root of why they're out there and trying to do things – we all love money and we all want it and we all need it. But if you're doing it for money, the day you fail or the days that don't go well or days you have to make certain decisions, you will be making those decisions for the wrong reasons and end up getting frustrated. Now, if you go into a business and you love it, if you don't – God forbid – ever make a dime out of it, were you happy every day seeing somebody wear your new product, feeling that new product that you're making, the excitement, you know? You can't sleep at night because you've got a new idea. That's exciting. And at least you were rewarded that way. Now, if you do that also, you're going to stay in that business way after all the people who were just there for money dropped out, - and you know what, you may actually succeed because you put so much time into it. So that's what I'm suggesting – you *have* to do it because you love it.

Not just for the money. Because, you know, after FUBU, everybody jumped on the bandwagon of creating clothing lines.

DJ: And you know, it's very, very hard.

Yeah.

DJ: It's very, very hard, especially now.

Especially now, Breaking in to the clothing – yeah, that's what I'm saying, it's oversaturated almost.

DJ: I don't even care about breaking into the clothing line; it's hard owning it, even at my level! (laughs) It's very right now. You know the economy we're at right now – people are challenged with having to pay their mortgages, the last thing they're doing is buying another shirt. They're just going to wear that one shirt they have ten more times.

That's true, Very true.

Kind of off the subject, but where can I get another FUBU suit? I've only been able to find one.

DJ: Well, we're putting them back out, um we're re-launching FB, and it's going to be out October-November. And I would say, by that time, suits will probably be out, I would say, February or March, once we get a handle and a feel on the new bloodline, the DNA of the line, we will produce suits that match the more mature feel of the line.

So what kind of stores are they going to be in? Like a Macy's or –

DJ: It'll start off in specialty stores first, and then they will grow to, um – oh, you talking about the suits? The suits will probably be in Men's Warehouse, Macy's, and things like that.

DJ: Yeah, people didn't realize how good the suits were and how big the suit business was for us, because you don't have any big logo all over it.

And the fit is good, too, I had my tailor fix it a little bit, but the fit was real good.

DJ: Good, I appreciate that. I'm wearing one right now, actually.

Wow. That's what's up. But um, I still have a pair of FUBU socks I've probably had since '97. And they're still good. (laughs) That's the funny part.

DJ: You know, that's what, on another topic, what we've realized – and this is really funny too, and I never thought of it – is that, we haven't made FUBU for eight years in the United States besides maybe some shoes, right? But you'll see a lot of product in the street, and the kids will go, "Ah man, that's wack, because… I don't care if it's Louis Vuitton or Gucci, if you look at what you bought from them 10-15 years ago, it does not look styled as in today's style. But if you buy Louis Vuitton and Gucci and you don't buy the higher-end product, like the $20,000 shelling leather coat, most of your Louis Vuitton and Gucci will fade or get old or rip up and you will discard it in 3-4 years. The FUBU stuff, people generally never discarded. What they would do was – a fly leather coat we used to make, like an $800 leather coat furnished lamb leather that Gucci would charge $4,000 for – if you're out of that style, you're at least giving it away to your younger brother or you're giving it away to the Salvation Army and a bum's going to wear it, but it's still looking crazy. So what we did is we emphasized so much quality, it made us look crazy after a while.

Yeah, that's true. I remember going and buying, you know, one of your tees. I think at the time, when they was in JC Penny's they were like thirty bucks, and my dad was like, "Dude, you just paid thirty bucks for a t-shirt," and he felt it and he said, "Oh, I see why this is thirty bucks."

DJ: Thanks.

There is a big difference is in the quality of your clothing, versus the others, like you said.

DJ: Yeah, and that's what we always felt. If you emphasize product quality, no matter what, the consumer cannot argue and the will get very excited – and the product is an investment.

Right, that's true. How did you come up with the new re-invention of FUBU, like you know the platinum FUBU with the Fat Albert, the Muhammad Ali – like was that some of your ideas, or did you have a team of designers to come up with things like that? How did you come up with things like that?

DJ: Well FUBU was, you know the thing about, for us as buyers, is because, you know, we were publicly recognized, people come up and give us ideas on the street and talk with us. So I can't say that I came up with an idea, or I don't know who came up with the idea, but um, you know every idea was, you know – the Iceberg was selling a lot of characters, you know, at that time, and Snoopy and those things. And we thought about, you know, it would be cool to throw in those cartoons that we like, you know, so we found Globetrotters, Ali, and Fat Albert, and that how we got on. And I don't recall who thought of the exact character or whatever it was, but that's how it happened, and we decided to distribute it and we killed the Iceberg doing that at the same time.

Yeah, y'all smashed them. You completely smashed them.

DJ: But it wasn't intentional, you know what I'm saying? It was the concept of the company, man. Iceburg was selling sweaters for $7-800 when we could make the same one for $250, why they doing that?

I forgot about Iceberg until you just said it, which is crazy. (laughs)

So, what do you think the number one key to success is?

DJ: Doing something you love. But let me, um, because that was already in the prior part of the interview – another important key is to really, really research, and most of the battles are won before you even get on the field, you know? So really do research in whatever you're trying to be successful at.

I saw on your Twitter that you said you've been unfocused for the last four days because you weren't reading your goals.

How important is it to continue to have goals, even when you reach a level of success?

DJ: There is no level of success that you'll reach where goals are not important, you know? I think Donald Trump and Bill Gates and Warren Buffet all have goals, and the goals don't necessarily have to be of a monetary aspect. But you know, you have to read your goals, I think that is very important in regards to life, um, you know because you're going to have a goal at a certain age to remain healthy, you know? That you love your family the way you should, you leave a legacy that is beneficial to the world, and a lot of other things. And I'm not trying to preach, I'm just explaining that the monetary aspects of goals are not necessarily the ones that are important, you know? But goal setting is very, very important.

Very true, So do you have any kids?

DJ: Yeah, I have two kids, yeah.

Are you raising them as entrepreneurs, or are you persuading them to go to school or maybe go down another path?

DJ: I persuade them to do whatever they want and let's see how it pans out – let's let their imagination run. And you know, they're pretty good kids. I just don't – I'm not saying that anything's wrong with it, I just don't necessarily agree with, um, putting – when notable people put their children in the public eye, and create a certain amount of pressure on the kids to be somebody or live the part of something, I don't agree with that.

I know what you mean. Kind of like, I don't know why this came to my mind, but like Michael Jordan's sons, you know, they both playing ball.

DJ: Yeah, you know, if the kid wants to do it, that's cool and, you know, and to me – if my kid wanted to do it, I would have to see that fire in that kid's eyes, for four, five, six years, on the same thing to want to do it. If they want to do it because they just want to be famous, I will not support it. But if my child was a singer, I would need to see four, five years of that child going to vocal lessons, singing, writing music, trying to improve their art, and I go, "Okay, this is not a fad and this is not, 'I just want to be famous,' this is 'I have a love for this.'" You know? And I also have to give them challenges, and say, "Okay, you want to be a singer? Okay, then I want you to go to the park today and just stand there and set up a microphone and a little bucket of money and I want you to sing." And if they don't want to do that because there are no lights, cameras, and actions, then they don't want to do it.

Right, and then that will separate if they love it or if they just like it.

DJ: Exactly. And, you know, I'm still what I consider very young, and I may be completely wrong in my assessment of how to handle it, but that's just, you know, that's how I look at things.

I agree with it. 100%. It's like, my sister wanted to act, and she wanted me to use some of my connections to help her get in to acting, and I said, "I want you to do this," I gave her a little test. And she didn't do it, and I haven't heard anything else about it. It's been a year, and she's hasn't been in acting.

DJ: Right. Maybe she'll come back, you know? And maybe she'll come back, and reality will hit her, and she's say that she's ready – and if she doesn't, she doesn't. But at least, you know, you'll be there for her, if she's ready or not.

That's true. I do that a lot in business, too. People will come to me with ideas of something they want to do, and I give them a project. And if they come back and handle that project, then we proceed. But most of the time people bring you something, and they want you to do it.

DJ: Oh, of course.

(laughs) I'm sure you get that a lot more. So how do you handle things like that?

DJ: The fact that people bring me something and they want me to do it?

Yeah, they want you to do it.

DJ: I'm too busy anyways, so by the time they realize that nothing's going anywhere, and I say, "Well, nothing's going anywhere because you didn't do anything," and you know, they either kind of fade away or step up their game and they get it to that point.

We were just talking about goals, and that you write down your goals. Do you mind sharing one of your goals?

DJ: Um, let me see one that I can share. Well, the way that I just explained setting goals, I would suggest anybody to do it would be to read *Think and Grow Rich* and they should read Brian Tracy's goals. And to explain one of the ways that goals work – it's not something that's daily, about to do something, you know, that week. That is was I call a task, you know?

Right.

DJ: Goals are – that's the long term. So, you could – I set all my goals basically about three months out. And then my three month goals, there's my five year goals, and my twenty year goals. And I have about seven goals, and all of them range from health, to business, to family. So if I would talk about my health goals, I'll explain it to you like this. Whenever you read a goal, to yourself, you have to read first of all what you want to accomplish, second of all how will you accomplish it, and by what date. And in between doing goals - and I guess, you know, we call it goals, but Russell Simmons will call it meditating, and there's so many other ways to say it, it takes anywhere from twenty minutes to a half an hour a day – you also have to visualize yourself at that completion of the goal. If you cannot visualize it, you cannot hit a target, you cannot see. So, if I were to break down my goal for eating healthy, I would basically say, you know, I will remain at a weight or get to my goal weight of whatever – 175 pounds by, you know, drinking eight glasses of water a day, not eating fried foods, you know, or whatever the case is, because that would jeopardize my health. Not eating past 8 pm at night and working out one time a day, five days a week – and I will accomplish this by November

31st. And that's basically how you read it, you know, and I could give out way more details. And when November 31st comes around, and you are at that weight that you feel you can reset your goals, and change it for a different weight or, you know, or change it for whatever the case may be, or reset it, and that's basically how I read my goals.

Well, thank you Daymond, I don't want to hold you up, I appreciate you doing this interview.

DJ: Alright, I appreciate it, thank you very much.

Thank you, man.

My Daymond John Key Takeaways

Takeaway 1 - How to focus on your goals and the importance of having goals. He broke it down. Number one you have to know what you want, how you are going to accomplish it, and by what date you are going to accomplish it. So it was very cool to see how he broke down the goals and he made reference to or related to Think and Grown Rich which if you haven't read it you need to go read it.

Takeaway 2 – Key To Success: This something I always tell people, and I was very shocked to hear that he shared the same opinion. I asked him this question what do you feel like the number one key to success is. He said, what I often tell people is, it is doing what you love. Now I do have to make this disclaimer. In doing what you love there are some consequences that come with that. Please note that right off the bat you are not going to be as successful at doing what you love, but like he said are you happy enough to just get the reward of someone wearing your product or someone using your product or two or three people having it. Will that drive you enough to keep going?

Takeaway 3 – A celebrity endorsement could ultimately make your company just as it did for Daymond. Plus how important it is to make those connections and get celebrities to endorse your products or have product placement into reality shows and different media forms. If you want a great example of this check out Donald Trump's Apprentice. A lot of the brands are embedded into the actual show. So it's another form of celebrity endorsement because they are able to attach their brand to Donald Trump because they are on Donald Trumps' Apprentice.

Takeaway 4 - Negotiation is all about the value seen in something versus what somebody sees. Meaning that negotiation is about me convincing you about the value I see in the product versus the opinion you might have about it. And **the first one to say a number always loses. It's a Fact!**

Takeaway 5 - Daymond was real cool and I enjoyed my interview with him. It was a dream come true. I used to ride around in FUBU from head to toe when FUBU first came out I had to have everything FUBU. That was pretty much my whole wardrobe. I didn't want to buy anything else. I didn't have anything else. All I wanted was FUBU, FUBU jeans, t-shirts, hoodies, hats, everything.

This relates to my previous point, it is all about that celebrity endorsement. Every time that I saw LL Cool J he had on FUBU. When he was on the VIBE cover he had on a red FUBU hoodie and a red FUBU hat. I said I had to have that and I went out and I got it. It was all about FUBU and even the tags on their clothing. I don't know if you all remember the original FUBU tags, but it had all the founders of FUBU on the tag and it had picture of them. I used to have that tag hanging on the vent in my car and I would ride around and see it every day. So it was a dream come true to actually talk to interview him.

Me & My Newborn Son In My FUBU Gear

Pic of my Fubu Hoodie LL Cool J had on in the VIBE
Magazine Cover Shoot! I had to have it!

Stuff To Know

What Is A Patent?

A patent for an invention is the grant of a property right to the inventor, issued by the United States Patent and Trademark Office. Generally, the term of a new patent is 20 years from the date on which the application for the patent was filed in the United States or, in special cases, from the date an earlier related application was filed, subject to the payment of maintenance fees. U.S. patent grants are effective only within the United States, U.S. territories, and U.S. possessions. Under certain circumstances, patent term extensions or adjustments may be available.

The right conferred by the patent grant is, in the language of the statute and of the grant itself, "the right to exclude others from making, using, offering for sale, or selling" the invention in the United States or "importing" the invention into the United States. What is granted is not the right to make, use, offer for sale, sell or import, but the right to exclude others from making, using, offering for sale, selling or importing the invention. Once a patent is issued, the patentee must enforce the patent without aid of the USPTO.

There are three types of patents:

1) Utility patents may be granted to anyone who invents or discovers any new and useful process, machine, article of manufacture, or composition of matter, or any new and useful improvement thereof;

2) Design patents may be granted to anyone who invents a new, original, and ornamental design for an article of manufacture; and

3) Plant patents may be granted to anyone who invents or discovers and asexually reproduces any distinct and new variety of plant.

To apply for a Patent and for More Info:
Go To: **www.uspto.gov/**

What Is A Trademark?

In short, a trademark is a brand name. A trademark includes any word, name, symbol, device, or any combination, used, or intended to be used, in commerce to identify and distinguish the goods of one manufacturer or seller from goods manufactured or sold by others, and to indicate the source of the goods. A service mark is any word, name, symbol, device, or any combination, used, or intended to be used, in commerce, to identify and distinguish the services of one provider from services provided by others, and to indicate the source of the services.

Must all marks be registered? No, but federal registration has several advantages, including a notice to the public of the registrant's claim of ownership of the mark, a legal presumption of ownership nationwide, and the exclusive right to use the mark on or in connection with the goods or services set forth in the registration.

To apply for a Trademark and For More Info:
Go To: www.uspto.gov/

What Is A Copyright?

Fundamentally, copyright is a law that gives you ownership over the things you create. Be it a painting, a photograph, a poem or a novel, if you created it, you own it and it's the copyright law itself that assures that ownership. The ownership that copyright law grants comes with several rights that you, as the owner, have exclusively. Those rights include:

• The right to reproduce the work
• to prepare derivative works
• to distribute copies
• to perform the work
• and to display the work publicly

These are your rights and your rights alone. Unless you willingly give them up (EX: A Creative Commons License), no one can violate them legally. This means that, unless you say otherwise, no one can perform a piece written by you or make copies of it, even with attribution, unless you give the OK.

Inversely, if you're looking for material to use or reuse, you should not do any of these things without either asking permission or confirming that the work is in the public domain, which means that the copyright has expired and all of the above rights have been forfeited. Simply put, if the work isn't in the public domain and you don't have permission to use a piece, you put yourself in risk of legal action, regardless of your intentions.

Because, beyond fair use and parody (issues for later essays), the holder of a copyrighted piece has near carte blanche to do what they want with their work. It's no different than owning a car, a house or a pen. One can lend it out to a friend, sell it, modify it or even destroy it. In short, if you own the copyright to something, you have the same rights that you do with anything else and, in some instances, even more. After all, you did create it. It only makes sense that you would own the fruits of your labor. That's what copyright law is all about.

To apply for a Copyright & for more info Visit: Copyright.gov

<u>Where You Can Find A Manufacture For Your Product?</u>

I don't care what time type of product you want to create, the first place I would look for a manufacture is **Alibaba.com**

I have used Alibaba.com to manufacture my latest product "The Thank You Lord Button" (www.thankyoulordbutton.com)

Short Cut Process To Private Label A Product

First what is Private Labeling? Private label products or services are typically those manufactured or provided by one company for offer under another company's brand. Private label goods and services are available in a wide range of industries from food to cosmetics to web hosting. They are often positioned as lower cost alternatives to regional, national or international brands, although recently some private label brands have been positioned as "premium" brands to compete with existing "name" brands.

Steps

1. Do Google Search for Private Label plus whatever it is you want to make. (Ex. Private label vitamins)
2. Review the results for the best suppliers.
3. Narrow your choices down to three.
4. Contact each provider and get all your questions answered about packaging, cost etc.
5. Choose the one that best fits what you are trying to do and that has the best customer service.

For Lovie Lip Gloss we chose lipbalmexpress.com they treated us like gold and was very excited about our project and had a very good price for the product.

Some of the things you want to be clear on is – price of the product production, will they drop ship your product for you to your customers, how much product you have to invest in upfront & shipping cost to you or your customer.

GREAT RESOURCES

Kelly Cole's Websites & Products

- PrimeTime-Marketing.com
- WebsiteFlipping202.com
- 30dayTakeover.com
- TheGeneratorClub.com

Other Sites To Check Out

- InTheSharkTank.com - #1 Shark Tank Blog On The Web
- DaymondJohn.com
- BarbaraCorcoran.com
- Mitchclarkphoto.com

Claim Your FREE Bonuses Now
www.conversationswithsharks.com/bonuses

Bonus Interview – with Steve from IWantToDrawACatForYou.com

Glad you showed up so let's jump right in to it, Tell us a little bit about yourself, where you from, how you got started and what are you doing now?

Sure I live in Evanston; I'm from the Chicago area. By day I build websites and by night I dream up crazy ideas and take them a little too far. So right now I'm a web developer full time and then I draw stick figure cats for people at night and I produce some comedy shows in Chicago as well.

Sounds great, I told you a little bit in the email I actually grew up in Chicago, I moved to Virginia my sophomore year of high school and I hated it but of course I had no choice I was still a minor and I ended up staying here and I'm still here now. As I got older this was actually a great place to raise kids and have a family cause I was living in the inner city of Chicago's crazy parts.

How did you come up with the crazy idea I want to draw a cat for you?

I just wanted a business so I thought, I didn't want the manufacturing side of the business, I wanted to do marketing and promotions and see what I could sell to people. So I took a product I could produce easily and that really didn't cost me that much to produce and that was just a stick figure cat you know I've been doodling since I was a little kid and then I just challenged myself. I said here's a stick figure cat, it's something nobody needs, nobody knows exist, how many of these can I get out and sell. I picked a little song and did a little dance and sold a bunch of these things.

So you wrote the song yourself?

Yea I did. I wrote the lyrics, I opened up garage band one day on the laptop and recorded it and that was it.

That thing sticks in your head; it's a very catching song. How many people told you you were crazy for putting up that website?

The people who know me already know I'm crazy so to them it was just another one of my silly projects. But anyone who didn't know or people I just worked with when I explained it to them they definitely just rolled their eyes at me I get this all the time people look at me and they look at the website and say you have too much free time and I hate hearing that because to me no I don't because I'm using that time to create stuff and usually people who say that you have to much free time on your hands you got to look and say what are you creating what are you doing with your free time.

Exactly, so the people who didn't know me thought this was stupid?

They expected I would sell a couple, but you know didn't think much of it beyond that.

Now you're over 2,000 sold.

Yea we've actually sold 3,400 of them so I've got this long queue of drawings so how you like me now right.

That's it rub it in your face.

Part of me wants to but I also understand that a lot of the success of this, most of the success of this right now is due to a reality television show and I know that without that this would still be the silly little side project and maybe it would of caught on in other ways but probably not at this scale so its success I can't pretend is all on me I'm always doing projects I do enough of them that sometimes the opportunity and the timing is right and something catches like this.

Right so before you went on Shark Tank you had sold quite a few?

Yea about 1,500 of them and that was helped a lot by Groupon, I'd approached them kinda as a joke and I said I sell this great product and I went through their application that day, you know that all retail places go through but my product was the stick figure cat and I thought they will get a laugh out of this but they said no let's do this and it was really successful and it sold out really fast. So they got their piece of it and it got a lot of press because it was such a strange idea and it was a win win for both of us it was great. I didn't make a ton of money and I had to draw a lot of cats but for me it was the publicity I needed to help me get on Shark Tank so it worked out you know.

That's great, so what's your favorite cat you ever drew? Do you have a favorite?

You know what I draw so many that gosh usually by the time I start one I've forgotten what the last one was(wow) yea it cause I go through so many of these and I'm breathing in all this sharpie marker and you know my head gets so dizzy. I would say there was some cool one a long time ago somebody wanted a George Washington cat crossing the Delaware, that was kind of an instinct, I'm not a good artist it's just part of the hook on this I can't really draw so when people ask for cats playing guitars or cats riding bicycles my brain has this mental block so it always ends up looking awful like so bad. So they think they're funny to just watching how much effort I had to put into making this terrible guitar with like hands kind of bent over backwards plucking strings and impossible bicycles with crooked legs so it's just kind of fun.

That is cool. So tell us about the process you took to get on Shark Tank. How did that thought come about?

For me I'm sure it was different then for most entrepreneurs. I, again just like with the Groupon thing I sent an email that was kind of a joke, I said I was watching the show and saw they were casting and sent them an email that said hey "I draw stick figure cats let me at those sharks" and that was it. I put a link in to the website and again I thought some casting agent is going to look at this and get a good laugh out of it and maybe he'll buy one or tell a friend. Then a couple weeks later they called me and asked me to create a video for them so I made a video and it was kind of a fun little video and I included clips from my dance from the website and then I think it was a month later I got another call and suddenly I was on the phone with them twice a week working on my pitch. The whole time they were saying we do this with a lot of people don't worry you might just stop hearing from us one day, and they just never stopped calling and we just kept working on it. And I think about a week before I flew out there is when they finally said ok you're coming out here's your itinerary. (Wow) And you get out there and they warn you every step of the way you might never appear on the show. You might not ever pitch with the sharks; you know it's all so tentative until you see yourself on television. So it was really a stressful experience but I had the time of my life out there too.

That's great stuff, what was your subject line of your email? I draw stick figure cats.

I don't remember the subject, it was probably let me on your show but the email was just two sentences, it was I draw stick figure cats let me at those sharks and I went to the website so you know maybe one of the pitfalls is if you send them to much information you have to remember the people looking at these submissions, they're not investors, you know their casting people. Their people with a day job who get bored with their day job and they want to have a little fun, so if you can catch their attention with something out of the ordinary maybe that's your best hook you know.

Right I got you. So what was it like once you got up there, what was it like standing in front of the sharks?

It was awesome , I thought I'd be nervous, but I wasn't at all you're there for a whole week kind of rehearsing, getting yourself ready, meeting the producers, and that to me that was the nerve racking part. I was very nervous for all that. But really I always had the idea that I was being asked out there for comic relief (right) but the producer never said that and they were very encouraging saying we think maybe you have a chance getting a deal but they have to tell me that right so I'll try right I get it they want me to do my dance they want me to rap and that's going to be funny because I'm not a rapper or a dancer. So I thought ok if I'm going to make an ass of myself on national TV I'm not going to do it half way. Well I'm here to have fun so what an opportunity to get to stand in front of these guys who look through deal after deal of legitimate businesses I almost felt like wow I'm pulling one over on everybody here so I just went all out and I wasn't nervous and it was so fun and I was so surprised I half expected ok this is the segment I do my pitch and one by one they all say nope, nope, nope, nope, nope and I just walk out the door. But when they started asking me legitimate questions, I was really taken by surprise I thought oh ok it must have been pretty nice.

When Kevin O'Leary went out and you told them hey this is the last thing you're going to remember when you lay your head down that was the best and they all laughed.

Yea I had been holding on to that line for months because I knew you know I'm like ok Kevin O'Leary, you know I've been watching the show and I wanted to set them up so bad and there's no way he's not going to go out and when he goes out I want to just haunt him. I want to remind him that this song is never going to go away, that he's going to say no but I already got it in his head you know your mine for good now. So I was so happy that I got the opportunity to do that, to say that to him and then I worried that they would edit it out, because there was enough footage in there to make me look really bad or make me look really smart however they wanted to do it you know. But I was really happy they left that in there.

Cool! So what made you take the deal with Mark?

Of all the people there, from the research I had done, I thought if anyone is going to invest in this I thought maybe I had an actual chance with him, if he can see that there is more to this and to me than just stupid ideas; that there is some creativity and some execution behind this. Not just anyone can do something this dumb and make it look so polished. So part of me to was, I had asked for ten thousand dollars for a quarter of the company and I expected ok they may say we'll give you ten thousand dollars but for fifty percent of the company, but when he more than doubled the money I was asking for and only bumped up the equity a tiny bit, I thought he must of made a math mistake or something he messed up but I better take this before he figures it out. Because I'm there with stick figure cats, if someone puts that kind of money on the table I'm gonna grab it before they come to their senses. His was the deal and then Daymond wanted to go in with him on it but Mark didn't want him in on it and as they were kind of doing cross talk I just kept thinking you know what I've seen this happen were you pause on this and it just disappears (right) I better just grab it.

They didn't show that part on the show where him and Daymond was trying to get together.

They showed one little line where Damon said interested and then they kind of cut a bunch of pieces and then tech is not going to fight for me but from what I remember and to be honest it all happens and you walk out of there and you don't remember anything that's just happened but I'm pretty sure he was trying to say wait let him go in on it with Mark and Mark was saying no you know what I don't need you as part of this. I already felt the thing changing and I didn't want anything to go away. (Exactly) so I turned around and said no, no Mark I do want to work with you.

Kind of like the guy that went from six hundred thousand to four hundred thousand tonight.

I felt so bad for him, I wanted him to take Kevin's deal, like his idea if I was brilliant and that product I want one of those and I feel bad that it is owned by these billionaires and that this guy isn't getting any money. Maybe Mark will send me a free one now since he own this company.

They got him pretty good I felt bad for him too.

Right and nobody wants to be that guy, I already made an ass of myself doing the dancing and the singing, so I want to look smart and take the money and run.

So what is it like working with Mark?

It's cool. I don't come from a business background so this is all really new to me and there's probably a lot of decisions I should be making on my own but I like to check in with him to make sure. Once you do Shark Tank there's so many things that come flying at you and I don't feel that I have the experience to really understand them or process them or look through them to see what's real and what's bologna so I shoot him an email from time to time. He's pretty responsive, pretty quick with his answers but he makes a lot of sense so its unlike anything I've ever done I've never worked with anyone like this before and for him this is a pretty small investment so it's not like he's thinking about it daily. But he's been good with his time; he's been responsive which is all I can really ask for.

Right, so he is a cool guy, he's not, he's not a jerk?

Yea, He has no problem telling me if he thinks something I say is stupid so that's fine too. He's only responds to stuff that he is genially into. He's doesn't sugar coat it.
Which is cool, I can respect that, I like people that shoot straight and don't feed you full of crap.
He's also like an alien too because he's a billionaire and I don't think they remember what it is to not be a billionaire so there's always that disconnect to you know.

Right, that's true too. How important do you think implementation is on, like implementing an idea, like do you think it is important to try them all? What is your process on the things you actually try and put out there?

I have a filter that I think is pretty good for what all my ideas are like a variety of something so stupid that it's funny. I have a lot more ideas that I don't follow through on that are so stupid, there stupid. I found success in following through on something all the way if you're going to start it so with this project and other ones its always to me about, if you think something sounds good you have to finish it, not just half do anything so I think the execution and implementing is very important.

Tell us about two film t-shits.com where did that come from?

After the cat stuff was happening, I was trying to think of other similar products and this one kept coming to me was what if we solve a problem that doesn't exist; which is let's make a commercial that shows oh no I like two films but I don't know how to express that without wearing two t-shirts and then have some magical guy appear and solve it, and says hears a t-shirt with two movie titles on it and then the world is right again. So it was an experiment, solving problems that don't exist and seeing what else and seeing what other funny video we can make and can we turn around and actually have that sell product. That hasn't been as successful but it's ahead of its time you know it's waiting for its audience.

I must say it's very cool though, I thought it was very creative.

Thank you

Two film t-shirts, I was like get out of here, and the people look cool wearing them too.

You'll see them everywhere soon. I sent one to Mark and I said Mark can you give me a picture of you wearing your two film t-shirt and he just said no.

What?

Yea he said no, so I don't know if that means he's not in to the product or what. Like I said he'll tell you straight, no I will not send a picture of me in that stupid shirt.

What two films was it?

I can't remember, if you look on the website you'll see it on the right column there's a shirt that will say it's in Mark C and Dallas ...

Did you ask him what his two favorite films were?

I said hey give me your address and your two favorite films and he sent those so he got his shirt.

Now on the show you said you get most of your ideas when you are in the restroom, do you keep an idea journal?

No, I say a lot of that was for TV, so they had me shoot some stuff in the shower. (Are you serious?) I'm glad the cut those showers out. But I had mentioned in the interview, you know when they say where you get these ideas. I said in the shower or in the bathroom. That parts true you know, I don't really keep a journal, but I'm usually quick to execute if something strikes me and I want to do it then I've got the domain in about ten minutes. You should see the list of domains that I own and all the projects that I haven't decided to execute on its kind of wacky. Sometimes I look at that list and I think oh man what was I thinking.

I finally went to rehab, I did not buy a domain unless I'm ready to implement now. Because after a while you've got all these domains and then it's time to renew them. Then you've got a decision to make. I've definitely stopped doing that, I know how that works. So, do you follow any marketers online, internet marketers?

No, you know why too, I think a lot of its snake oil, I don't buy a lot of it. You know a lot of the stuff I see out there gets me really frustrated because I think beyond all that beyond search engine optimization, and all these little marketing tricks, it's all content, if you create something that's entertaining that's it. I mean there's no substitute for that. I think clean websites and that kind of stuff is important. I don't buy into search engine optimization, and I think if you're making money with it you're just tripping you're way into money and it's not real. I don't buy into the tricks about building giant twitter followings or Facebook followings I think it's about connecting with engaged customers, and if you have ten engaged customers that's better than ten thousand unengaged customers so I think it's about genuine communication and creating a product that connects with people and then connecting with people as they purchase and that to me that's just what instinct tells me, so that's what I do I don't get caught up in that stuff, I don't read many books on it or follow anybody on it. You know I shoot kind of from the gut and I'm happy to make mistakes and kind of learn from those and I think to me that's more valuable. I don't mean to diminish people who do that I think some people learn best that way but for me the best way for me to learn is by screwing up, learning from my mistakes, kind of stumbling my way through it. I found the projects that I do that are more successful are the ones I passionate about regardless of how I market them or position them. You know the cat drawing thing I felt like I actually wanted to draw cats for people. I wanted people to email me request and I wanted to draw something on a piece of paper and send it to them because that to me is a very classic form of communication and it gives me a thrill, so that was enough for me to grow this; plus being on a reality show helped too.

That's good stuff. So you didn't do any type of press or anything other Groupon when you started drawing cats?

Yes I do press, the other stuff I do is all pretty decent stage shows so I kind of have my network of press contacts for that stuff so that kind of helped usually from here, at a point though the press was coming to me which was cool with this one you know Groupon helped a lot too. Suddenly it became a story when some idiot from Chicago had to draw a thousand cats because he stupidly offered up a Groupon for them, but that all turned into great press too.

Alright I'm not going to hold you anymore, I have one last question. What do you feel the key to success is?

I think the key to success is, and I think this will sound really trite, but it's to be yourself. You know I think, when people succeed, they're succeeding by doing things that are an extension of them and not trying to you know do things they're not comfortable with and that kind of goes back to what I just said to about if you're doing something you're passionate about, then you have an actual deeper connection to than trying to make money with it than that will drive you to succeed.

But I just draw stick figure cats; I don't really know what I'm talking about.

You do, you sold over three thousand stick figure cats so you definitely know what you are talking about.

Well, I appreciate that.

Thank you so much for doing this interview. I had a great time.

Thanks for having me,

Steve's Website: www.Iwanttodrawacatforyou.com

Twitter.com/CatDrawingGuy

Be Sure And Download Your Free Bonuses Here:
conversationswithsharks.com/bonuses

ABOUT THE AUTHOR

I'm Kelly Cole a.k.a. The Generator, I'm a minister. I'm a husband. I'm a father of three. I'm a full-time internet marketer. I provide for my family with my online business. To give you a brief history about myself, I worked at WalMart for eight years, I hated every minute of it. The only thing I liked about it was that they cut the checks on time. It was a definite paycheck every two weeks.

I was a slave to their company. They controlled my Destiny. They told me what to do, when I could eat, when I could have off, and if I could go to my son's basketball games, football games. Thank God, now that I work for myself and run my business online, I can do pretty much anything I want.

On Sunday evenings after we went to church and Sunday dinner, I and my family started a tradition to go to the bookstore to buy books or magazines.

One Sunday me and my family were in "Books A Million", and I saw a magazine sticking up out of the magazine rack and it said, "Web Made Millionaire" and it kind of struck me so I begin skimming through it and reading it. What I was reading was so electrifying, it captivated me; I immediately decided I wanted to quit Wal-Mart and start my own business online from home. But things don't happen quite as fast as we want; sometimes we have to build our faith up to get to the point where God wants us.

So what I did was punk out for another year and didn't step out on my faith and didn't do what God called me to do. So one night a year later, I was watching the movie The Pursuit of Happiness, if you haven't seen it Will Smith played a guy named Chris Gardner and told his story. By the end of the movie when Chris Gardner got the job and after he went through all what he did, I was crying.

I told God I said that even if I end up like Chris Gardner, If I end up in the bathroom stall, I said I am going to trust you I'm going to step out here and I am going to do this thing on faith. I made up in my mind, I'm going to do it, I'm going to quit.

The next day I went back to work, Wal-Mart told me they We're going to send me to Arkansas for a week for what was called a shareholders meeting. So I said great, this is going to be a good time to get away, to travel and they were paying for everything. So I said cool of course. I got to Arkansas and got checked into my room.

The next day we had all these different events we could go to, so I went to this one meeting, I walk in and all of the sudden the real Chris Gardner from the movie The Pursuit of Happiness was walking towards me. Immediately I recognized the spirit of God, he put both of us in this same place at the same time and I knew I was walking towards my destiny just by that happening. That was not a coincidence it was truly the hand of God.

God showed me where he took Chris from and where he was taking me and at that point in our lives he put us in the same place so immediately I knew that God was calling me to do my own thing. So when I came back home I decided I was going to do it; put in my two weeks' notice.

God said don't do it now, your last day can't be until July 15th and I didn't understand that but I went ahead I said alright I'm going to wait because God said July 15th. So the next Friday night I'm watching TBN and Bishop Walker III is hosting and he's got Bishop Bloomer on. Bishop Bloomer he's in the spirit and he's going off and he's saying the angels of the Lord are here right now, they're right now in your living room doing that thing you want them to do, that thing is done, whatever you're believing God for is done he said I don't care if its July 15th, that thing is done. So immediately you know what I did I began to get up to praise God, I got up jumped and shouted and praised God. I fell out in the spirit.

You know what was so real and amazing about that is what God did was reach inside me and confirmed something and he touched me that night. I will never forget that night. So the next day at work, I put in my notice to quit on July 15th and I told God there was no way I could turn back, after him revealing that to me in my life. I have never looked back since, I have been online ever since making money, selling products, develop websites, and helping other people develop websites and provide income with their passion online. There was no way I could have told God no, once I asked him to come on the water and he told me to come. There was no way I could turn back and tell him no. My personal relationship with God has grown tremendous throughout this whole process. I want to encourage you to trust God and have faith and he can do the same in your life. Don't worry about the circumstances just trust him and keep your eyes on him. If you begin to sink cry out and ask him to save you and he will.

Kelly Cole is currently available for corporate, nonprofit, faith-based, and educational (middle/high school & college) speaking engagements, panel discussions, workshops & keynotes.

<u>Topics Include but not limited to</u>:
Cash-In With Your Passion
5 Steps Finding Your Purpose
Staying Motivated To Achieve Your Goals
How To Use Your Gift To Produce Income Online
Cash While In College
Internet Entrepreneurship For Youth & Young Adults
Product Creation
Publish A Book In 2 Weeks!
For Booking email: info@conversationswithsharks.com

Be Sure and Download Your Free Bonuses Here:
www.conversationswithsharks.com/bonuses

Made in the USA
San Bernardino, CA
17 December 2013